I Wrote on All Four Walls

I Wrote on All Four Walls

TEENS SPEAK OUT ON VIOLENCE

EDITED BY FRAN FEARNLEY

Annick Press
Toronto ✶ New York ✶ Vancouver

We acknowledge the support of the Canada Council for the Arts, the Ontario Arts Council, the Government of Ontario through the Ontario Book Publishers Tax Credit program and the Ontario Book Initiative, and the Government of Canada through the Book Publishing Industry Development Program (BPIDP) for our publishing activities.

Cataloging in Publication

   I wrote on all four walls : teens speak out on violence / edited by Fran Fearnley.

Includes bibliographical references.
ISBN 1-55037-757-4 (bound).—ISBN 1-55037-756-6 (pbk.)

   1. Youth and violence. 2. Violence in adolescence. I. Fearnley, Fran

HV9069.I2 2004   303.6'0835   C2004-903379-4

The text was typeset in Apollo.

Distributed in Canada by: Published in the U.S.A. by Annick Press (U.S.) Ltd.
Firefly Books Ltd.   Distributed in the U.S.A. by:
66 Leek Crescent   Firefly Books (U.S.) Inc.
Richmond Hill, ON   P.O. Box 1338
L4B 1H1   Ellicott Station
                                   Buffalo, NY 14205

Printed and bound in Canada by Friesens, Altona, Manitoba.

Visit us at:
www.annickpress.com

oN all Four Walls: TeeNs SPeak Out oN VioleNce I Wrote oN all Four Walls: TeeNs SPea
N VioleNce I Wrote oN all Four Walls: TeeNs SPeak Out oN Wrote oN ra
Walls: TeeNs SPeak Out oN VioleNce I Wrote oN all Four Walls: TeeNs SPeak Ou
eNce I Wrote oN all Four Walls: TeeNs Out oN VioleNce Wrote oN all Fou
TeeNs SPeak Out oN VioleNce I Wrote oN all Four Walls: TeeNs SPeak Out

CONTENTS

Foreword

Here are the voices of youth. The stories may be difficult, but they are true and they have a power that comes with truth.
Readers may be surprised to learn that this book has its beginnings in the Toronto Public Library (TPL). Listening and responding to youth is a priority for the Library. This may be the first book of young voices that the Library has made commercially available, but it has grown out of a library tradition that seeks to give voice to the stories, thoughts, and poems of youth. TPL's annual publication *Young Voices* was launched in the 1970s; since that time it has celebrated the creative efforts of teens living in the city.

In 1999, the Toronto Public Library made a commitment to reach deeper into the teen community, creating a new publication, *Young Voices from the Street*. "Squeegee kids," "homeless youth," and "street kids" were phrases that the public was hearing on the radio, reading about in the papers, and quickly growing tired of. The mainstream media featured few if any positive images of this segment of the population, and TPL seized the opportunity to bring a positive approach to the issue of street youth. Annick Press recognized the power and immediacy of the writing in the publication. So when TPL— through its Children and Youth Advocate, Ken Setterington— decided to continue to seek the raw and oftentimes edgy voices of youth discussing violence, Annick agreed to bring this publication to a wider audience.

The words *teens* and *violence* are often linked in the media. However, most often teens are the victims of violence, and the voices of young victims are seldom heard. The Toronto Public Library with assistance from the City of Toronto, through the Children and Youth Action Committee, has sought to provide a forum for youth to express their thoughts about violence.

Here are the powerful stories of youth who agreed to share their experiences and their stories. Listen to their voices. Read their stories.

Josephine Bryant
City Librarian, Toronto Public Library

Preface

We heard from many, many more young people than the nine who share their stories in this book. Not surprisingly, we discovered violence is hard to talk about honestly and constructively—whether you are the victim or the aggressor. It's not that we were looking for happy endings, but we wanted readers to hear from those who—even if they were still struggling—had insights to share. The overarching observation from all the youth we listened to is that violence changed, forever, the way they experience the world.

We made some observations too. Girls found it easier to talk about their feelings and responses, and to get beyond describing the events in order to explore the underlying reasons for their own behavior and to see how they might move forward. Fewer boys volunteered to share their stories and those who did were often not ready to make themselves vulnerable. They mostly spoke of the violence they experienced with bravado or in a detached way. The young men whose voices you hear in this book, however, have reached a point where they are prepared to face what violence has done to them and the complex responses that emerged by going through that process. More power to them.

Adam, Allan, Caitlin, Claire, Debbie, Don, Janice, Kevin, and Sue told us about their encounters with violence in one-on-one taped interviews. Their very own words, transcribed from those interviews, are what you will read. My role was to keep their words and their personalities intact while helping their stories flow sequentially and editing out the transgressions and repetitions we all make when we speak. These are their authentic oral testimonies as told to an empathetic adult listener.

Bullies; victims; those who have been both; aggression at home, in school, and on the street; abusive intimate relationships; gay bashing; parents who punish with violence; gang fights; intimidation— they are all here. These are topics we are all too familiar with. While the horror of the Columbine shootings stands out like a lightning rod (it's no coincidence that in two of the testimonials, which involved encounters with the police, officers make reference to the Columbine tragedy), "teen violence" is a recurring theme in the media.

Adults with a range of backgrounds, from psychologists to community leaders, are frequently invited to comment on the issue of violence and youth. The insights of caring adults, however valuable, are nevertheless one step removed. *I Wrote on All Four Walls* brings the voices of the youth themselves into the discussion. It's an important and powerful contribution and one that their peers and adults need to hear. We invite you to listen.

Fran Fearnley

Acknowledgments

First of all, our thanks to the many youth who volunteered to share their experiences with us, whether or not their stories were selected for publication.

Thanks also to Jasmine Miller and Teresa Pitman, who gathered these oral testimonies in one-on-one interviews. It was a delicate and often challenging task to gain the trust of these young people so that they felt secure enough to tell their stories.

There were many individuals, agencies, and organizations that helped to connect us to youth who had experienced violence. Special thanks are due to Eve-Lynn Stein, who was particularly helpful in this regard.

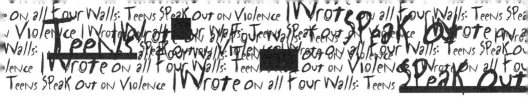

Sue

Sue's struggles with family instability, substance abuse, stealing, gangs, violence, and restrictive cultural traditions instilled in her the strength to face the ugliness of the world and to strive for a better life.

I'm 17. I have an older brother; he's 11 years older than me. I grew up in mainland China, in the country. My mom and dad got divorced when I was three years old. I can remember my parents fighting all the time. I was standing there, watching. Both of them were crying. I was so young I didn't know what to do.

My mom moved out because at that time in China, when you went to court and divorced, the husband had to buy a home for the wife. So my dad bought an apartment for her. She moved there and half the furniture went to her because my dad was rich at that time.

The reason why my dad divorced my mom, from my understanding, is because my mom looked old and ugly and my dad had become rich and wanted someone young and beautiful. Then he could go out and people would say, "Oh, look at that guy. He's got all the money and a beautiful girl!"

After the divorce, the government saw my dad had money, so they decided he could have both his children. Both my brother and I went to live with my father. My father sent my brother to a different province to go to the best school in China. I stayed home with my dad.

The hardest thing was that I missed my mom a lot, but my

13

dad wouldn't let me go see her. He didn't believe I should stay in contact with her after the divorce. He was scared that my mom would try to take me away from him. Back then my dad was a guy who wanted to be successful. He taught me to sit like a princess. I had to sit straight, with my legs closed. If there was no table in front of me, I had to sit with my legs crossed. When I ate, I had to sit straight. It just felt like it was too much for me.

My dad's house was huge. On the first floor there was a beautiful garden. My grandpa lived on the first floor with my grandma because Chinese people believe in living with their parents—caring for their parents. On the second floor my brother's room was over on the right side. My father's room was the biggest room in the whole house. My room was just a corner.

We had a dog, a German shepherd, watching the house. We had security guards living there as well. They watched the house because, at that time, our house had cars, motorcycle, all kinds of things, because we had a lot of money.

My dad remarried three times. I didn't like any of them because they were very young. They could have been my sisters, or my brother's girlfriends. I couldn't stand them. When I'd talk to them, they'd say, "The reason why I'm with your dad isn't because he's cute. He's ugly. The reason I'm with him is because he has money and he buys me stuff." I was young, so when I'd tell my dad, he'd never believe me. He'd always beat me up and tell me to fuck off.

My father beat me all the time because I'd fight with my stepmothers. When they'd tell me they didn't like my dad, that they were just with him for his money, right then I had to force myself to grow up so as to protect my family, to protect my dad from them. Every single night I'd have nightmares about them trying to kill my dad and take over his money and our house. I was just scared of them. I would swear at them. If they tried to take me somewhere, I just took off. People said I was the worst kid around there because of the way I treated my stepmothers.

Then my dad couldn't take it any more. He said, "That's it! You're going to live with your mom!" I was happy. I wanted to live with my mom. I didn't want to see my dad with younger girls, making out.

Then I went to live with my mom. She said to my dad, "The only reason I will take her is because you pay me $800 a month to take care of her." My dad said, "OK," so I went to live with my mom.

I was about seven when I moved in with my mother. She had remarried. She was really mean to me. We'd fight every single day about TV. I was young. I liked to watch cartoons. She'd say, "You grow up. You don't need to watch cartoons. That's so immature." From that moment I hated cartoons. To this day I still don't like cartoons.

I always fought with my stepfather until I just gave up and my mother sent me back to live with my father again. I lived with my father for a year, then he sent me back to my mom. My mom was remarried again, to a different guy. He and I didn't get along either. He was talking about bad stuff, controlling my mom, beating my mom up. I couldn't stand anyone beating my mom up, so every time he'd try to lay hands on her, I'd grab him and kick him and stuff.

I remember one day my mom got angry and said, "Why are you getting involved in my life? If he wants to beat me up, it doesn't matter. I love him. You shouldn't get involved with my life. You aren't even my child!"

I said, "What do you mean, I'm not even your child?"

She said, "You're adopted. You weren't even our real child!" I asked where my real parents were and she said, "We don't know. We found you in a basket in the lake, floating around. We picked you up because we'd lost our second son and wanted a daughter, so we kept you."

That was the biggest shock for me. I ran to confront my father. He said, "That's not true. You are our real child." I didn't know who to believe, so I started searching out my real identity. I started asking all the neighbors. They all freaked. They said, "We can't tell you. You have to ask your parents." I said, "Why?" and they said, "We can't. Your father is the most powerful man in this place. We can't do anything behind his back. We'll get burned."

People were saying I was the devil's child, how I came and tried to destroy their families, tried to take over their money … all this bad stuff.

At that time my brother came back from school to live with us. When he moved home, he was into video games. He'd play them all the time. He'd skip school, not go to class. My dad would be chasing him down the road in the car. He'd beat him up and drag him home.

I started getting hooked on video games too, because of my brother. My dad got pissed off and smashed the video game. As he stepped over the mess, he said, "I'll never buy another video game, for no one!"

Other times my dad would beat me up for no reason. If he got mad at work, he'd take it out on me. Sometimes he'd use a big stick. Sometimes he'd hit me so hard that I'd bleed and I wouldn't be able to sleep on my back because my butt was hurting.

At that time in China it was OK to beat kids. Everybody did it. We had no rights, so we couldn't tell anybody. I was always told to keep family business within the family, so I never told anybody what was going on.

My grandpa was actually the closest person to me at that time. Every morning at six o'clock in the summertime, he'd knock on my door and say, "Hey, are you awake yet? Come downstairs with me and have a coffee or a tea and I'll tell you a story." So, every morning at six o'clock I would get up and go sit in the garden and drink coffee or tea and talk to my grandpa. He'd tell me about all the fairy tales and how they came to be. I loved him so much.

When I got older, I had to go to Grade 1 and my dad sent me to a different boarding school for that, also one of the best schools in the city.

I had two best friends in the whole school. We were really close. One day one of the girls changed. She started beating me up and bossing us around. She started teaching us to steal and do all crazy stuff. One day she took us to the bathroom and started banging our heads against the wall. Then, in Chinese, she said to us, "You want to live? Or die?" In Chinese the word "live" sounds like you have to go jump in the lake and the word "die" sounds like you have to go eat shit. We didn't know which one to choose, so I said, "I want to live." She said, "OK, let's go. You have to jump in the lake." I said, "No, I'm not doing it." Then, by accident, I stepped on her shoe. She said, "Lick it off!" I was so embarrassed, but I had to do it.

After that, school wasn't the greatest for me. I stopped being friends with that girl and the other girl's Grades started to drop, so she stopped being friends with me.

I met a new friend. She had a hard life too. She told me all about her problems. One day I saw in the newspaper that she had committed suicide because she couldn't handle it any more. That's where I got the idea for suicide. I cried and cried and cried because I lost her. I missed her so much. I still miss her. I thought, if she could do it, why couldn't I commit suicide? That's when I started to cut myself. When I first started, it really hurt. I was scared. I wondered what would happen to my family and what would happen to me. Would I be a ghost floating around? Will I go to hell? Will I go to heaven? But I didn't really care because my life was so bad, so I just kept cutting myself.

I felt so much better after I cut myself. I realized then that I wasn't trying to kill myself, I just wanted to cut myself. That's a big difference. Cutting myself made me feel better because the physical pain blocks the emotional pain. I continued cutting myself every single day.

The morning after my twelfth birthday, at about six o'clock, my dad woke me up. It was so early. I asked why he woke me so early and he said we were going on vacation. I said, "This early in the morning, we're going on vacation?" and he said, "Yes, we're going to Canada!" I said, "I've never heard of it. What's it like?" My dad said he'd buy me a book to read about it. I said, "OK. Are we coming back?" He said we'd come back, probably in a month or so. I thought, Cool! No more school! I hated school and was happy to get out of it.

I packed some of my stuff but not all of it. I didn't grab all my journals because I thought I was coming back. When I got in the car with my dad, he gave me a book about Canada. The book was written in Chinese and it was saying that everyone in Canada lived in igloos because it was so cold. I was like, "Holy! I'm gonna live in Canada for a month?!! That's crazy!"

We got on an airplane for a couple of hours which took us to Beijing, then another flight for a few hours which took us to Canada.

We stayed at a hotel for a week or so while we were looking for an apartment and registering me in school and everything. About two weeks later my dad said, "Bye." I was like, "What do you mean, 'bye'? I'm going with you." He said, "No. You're staying here." I said, "You said we were going on vacation," and he said, "Well, I meant to tell you that you're going to live in Canada." I said, "I didn't even say goodbye to my mother or my grandfather or my friends! Why would you let me leave like that?" He said, "The reason I didn't tell you is because if you had told all your friends that we were getting out, the Chinese government would have held us there. They wouldn't have let us go and we'd have been in a lot of trouble." I was so upset. I said, "Fine. Leave."

He said, "Don't worry. Your brother will take care of you." I'd never, in my whole 12 years, lived with my brother, so I asked my dad how he thought we'd suddenly be able to live together. He said, "You'll be fine. You're brother and sister!" In my head I was thinking, "We're not blood relatives" because that's what my mom told me.

My dad got on a plane and left.

From my understanding, the main reason we came to Canada was because my dad owed the Chinese government a lot of money. If they couldn't get the money from him, they might come after his kids and we'd be in danger.

My brother and I had a basement apartment in Vancouver at that time. It was near my elementary school. At first my brother was cooking for us, washing all the laundry—everything. He also went to school. My dad was still sending money to support us until he got really, really broke. Then my brother had no choice but to go to work. He would get home at exactly 4:30.

One day he said, "I'm not cooking for you any more. You're old enough to cook. I have to work, I have to go to school, I have to do all these things to support the family. Why don't you do something? All you do is go to school and sit on your butt watching TV." I said, "OK, I'll cook." He said, "OK, starting now, school finishes at 3:10 and you have to come home right away, go grocery shopping, and cook dinner by

4:30 when I come home. Then, after I eat, you're going to wash all the dishes, do all the laundry, and clean the house up."

At that time I wanted to do it because I wanted to take some of the stress off my brother—but it didn't really work. He'd come home from work and be angry. He'd say, "I hate my life. My boss is rude to me, I'm getting stepped all over …" I tried to comfort him and tell him things would be all right, but he'd yell, "It's not all right, and having you around, bugging me all the time …" and that was when he started beating me up.

He just slapped me across the face at first. Soon, though, he started pinching me, punching me, and kicking me on the floor. I was so, so angry, but I couldn't tell anyone. In China we were taught family business is family business! Don't tell anyone.

I didn't tell anyone. I'd just go to school all upset, crying all the time. I'd talk to my teacher, but I wouldn't really say anything.

We moved a lot. We lived in so many places. I had to change schools all the time. He constantly beat me up just for the hell of it. Any time he wasn't happy, or if I didn't cook a meal just right, he'd get upset. I had to learn 20 new words in English per day. I had to memorize the words and the spellings. If I couldn't do it, he'd beat me up. He was so crazy.

Then I met a church person and I wanted to go to church. At that time I believed in Buddha, but I'd met a Christian, so I wanted to go to church. My brother stopped me, saying, "Never mind that white gospel baloney. There is no God." He didn't believe in anything and he didn't want me going anywhere. I had to stay home 24/7.

One day I wanted to buy a bible, so I ran to get one, but I didn't know which one to buy because there were a lot of different kinds there. It took me a couple of hours to pick one, and by the time I got home, it was about 5:30 and I hadn't cooked dinner or anything yet. On the way home I was praying, "Please God, please forgive me. I didn't cook or anything and I know it's my fault, but please don't let my brother beat me." I walked so slowly because I was so scared to go home. When I got home, I just stared at my brother and he just stared back at me. He didn't hit me. I was so happy. I thought, "Oh my God, prayer works!"

Then I wondered if I'd just had good luck that day. The next time I was late home, I prayed and I didn't get beat up then either. After that I started going to church on Sundays, behind my brother's back. I told him I was going to do volunteer work. He found out one day, though, and he beat the hell out of me. He said, "Starting now, everywhere you go, I want to know the name, phone number, and address." I couldn't go to church any more.

One day when I went to school I had a black eye and my arms were all bruised up and I had blood on the back of my shirt, from my brother beating me. Plus I had cuts on my arms. I still have the scars. At that time I had a best friend named Annie. She was going through the same stuff as I was, so we trusted each other. We told each other everything. There was a teacher that Annie trusted, so we decided to tell her. We didn't know that teachers were obligated to report it if they were told about violence at home.

We told the teacher. The teacher called the cops and the cops called Social Services. That's how I got involved with Social Services, when I was 13.

I had to go live with foster parents. I hated it. For my whole life I'd had to take care of myself. Now suddenly there are two foster parents, three foster brothers, and one foster sister to help take care of me. I hated it. My foster mother was so strict. She wouldn't allow me to go to church, either. She had people following me around everywhere. She didn't want me dating anyone older than me, anyone younger than me, anyone that wasn't in my class, in my school.

She wasn't violent, but she really got on my nerves. I tried running away. We got into arguments all the time. She just pissed me right off. I couldn't do it any more. I just kept telling the social worker that I wanted to leave. They wouldn't move me, though, for a year and a half, until my foster mother kicked me out finally, because she said I punched her. I don't remember anything about punching her, though, because I was taking more than 40 pills, so my mind was messed up and I couldn't remember anything I did. She didn't have any bruises or anything, but she said, "I'm not going to charge you, but you get out of my house."

I moved back to Vancouver temporarily, then they finally found me a group home. I was 14, almost 15. I liked the house at first. I had my own room, there were only four girls living in the whole house, we had nice stuff ... but things got worse because my marks dropped down, I started dropping out of school.

I had too much stress to handle. I'd started working at the Cineplex. My new foster mom started blaming me for things I hadn't done. For example, if the house money got lost, she'd say, "I know you took it. Why are you blaming the other kids? They've been here longer, we know them ..." I was angry. I said, "You can't say that. You have no proof. You can search my room." She said, "Money is small and easy to hide. How would I be able to find it?" I said, "You shouldn't judge me." She insisted that I had done it.

A couple of months later we finally saw which girl was doing it.

One time a water pipe got broken. She said I'd done it and told me I was grounded until I admitted it. I was grounded for weeks and weeks. I'd rather have the punishment than confess to something I didn't do. She finally relented and let me off.

Finally they moved me again, to a new group home. I liked the new home. They were nice until I became violent. I decided to become violent.

I decided to just not give a damn about anything. I joined a gang and I became violent, I started smoking cigarettes, I started smoking weed, I started drinking more often. If anyone said anything about me, I'd just say, "Wanna fight? Wanna get into my face? You don't know who you're messing with!"

I got into fights a couple of times, but I didn't get charged. Lucky me. I started carrying a knife around with me. For protection. I felt I needed protection from everyone in the world. I really didn't trust anyone. It still takes me a long time to trust someone. Last year, in August, I started dating this black guy and he took me to his friends' house and his friends raped me. After that, there was no way I was going to trust anybody again.

Then I started dating this guy named Mike. He is the only guy I ever trusted. I told him everything about my life. I hadn't told anyone else except my best friend about my life. I told Mike everything I'd been through—everything. He helped me. He supported me. He's the only reason that I live in this world. I was madly in love with him. Then he broke up with me in January.

I just suddenly broke down. My body broke down. I had no reason to live. I had no family here—except my brother—any friends, I hated life so much that I decided to suicide. I went to one of the worst areas of the city. I decided to go there to get myself killed. I was there for hours and hours. No one seemed to want to beat me up. No one seemed to want to hurt me.

Finally I decided I couldn't do this any more. I had a ring

with me from my ex-boyfriend which I had bought for him but I had because we'd broken up. I went up to this guy and asked if he knew anywhere I could get poison. I told him I'd give him my ring and my chain, which were worth more than $100. He said he only knew about crack but that, if I took enough, I'd die because I'd never taken it before. I said, "OK, give me crack and I'll give you all I have."

We started walking down the street. He saw this drug dealer and talked. Then he took me to this place and smoked with me. Then he took me to this underground club and we went drinking.

The next morning when I woke up, he raped me. This time I decided not to charge anyone any more. I was sick and tired of charging people. I just left and called my ex. He came and took me to the hospital. We talked and talked and finally got back together.

He's a Muslim. He's half Spanish, half Afghan. He told me he couldn't be with me because I wasn't a Muslim. I told him I'd change my religion for him. He said, "My parents won't like the way you dress." I told him I was willing to dress the way they dressed, with the thing covering my face, covering my hair, covering my whole body. I didn't mind. I was willing to put my life on hold for him, that's how much I loved him.

He was part of the Afghani-For-Life gang. I was in a gang called Blue Dragon which is mostly Chinese people with a mix of some other people. I joined when I moved to Vancouver, when I moved to the group home. We basically—I've never done it personally—steal cars, take the engines, and sell them to people. That was part of the business that my ex was doing with us. We'd steal the car and get the engine, then sell it to them. They'd sell it to someone else for more money, or we'd make parts out of it.

Then we'd go beat people up. For example, one person beat up my buddy in the gang. Whether or not I wanted to get involved in revenge, I had to because he was my buddy. I had to fight anyone who was against my gang, against my people. We'd be beating up people on the street, laughing at old ladies walking by … I know that was wrong, but I had to fit into the group. I had no choice.

I wanted to be in the gang to make me powerful, to make me feel stronger, to make me a bad girl. I figured if I couldn't be a good girl, why couldn't I be a bad one? Whenever I did good things, nobody appreciated it; nobody cared. So I started to be bad. I beat people up, I did all these drugs, I helped people sell them, I helped people with counterfeit bills, we stole cars … We did crazy stuff until I just couldn't do it any more.

Something inside me just kept saying, "You want to live your life like a gangster? You want to have one of your children grow up to be ashamed of you? Do you want your parents to be ashamed of you after they'd spent all their money to bring you to Canada, after they spent all their energy bringing you up, even though you're not their real child?"

I had to get out. I tried, but gang members don't let you get out easily. They beat me up, they followed me everywhere. I could not tell anyone. I told people I had fallen down or that it was an accident from a play fight. I couldn't tell anyone the truth. I would have gotten killed. I was scared—terrified. I didn't know who to talk to.

I had changed my name (not legally) to Sue. People knew me as Sue. Somehow they just stopped chasing me. I don't even know why. I don't even know what happened to the people from the gang. I don't see them any more.

I had so much to handle, but I still managed to do it. I said to myself, "Would you rather make it or lose it? You'd rather die as a coward who never tried or would you rather die as a tryer or as a failure?" I decided to try with my life, no matter how bad it got.

Sometimes I did get depressed. I'd try and try and try and it wouldn't work out. I'd say, "To hell with it!" and I wouldn't try any more. Then something would always come into my mind and I'd say, "Sue, you can't give up. You're almost 18. You're almost an adult. Why give up now?"

I'm in part-time school now. Grade 11 English. I was supposed to be at full credit at the beginning of the school year, but I dropped out and went down to one credit because I couldn't handle it.

I'm trying to find a job. I live in another group home. I love this group home. It's pretty cool, but people steal stuff a lot.

I still use violence to solve problems, but I don't beat people up for no reason. For example, the day before yesterday I went to my old group home to visit. I was walking down the street and these two black girls wanted to beat me up just because of the way I look. I said, "You know, I don't want to fight. Leave me alone." They said, "No, we want to fight." I said, "No. It's wasting my time." They just started punching me. I can't just stand around and do nothing, so I had to fight back. My arm's still sore now. My back was bruised and everything.

I still use violence to solve problems, but it's less than before. I don't fight innocent people. I only fight when someone punches me. I have to protect myself. Otherwise, I'm OK.

I sometimes talk to my brother, but not often. My parents still live in China. I speak to them once a year. I don't know if I will see them again. I kind of miss them a lot, really, especially my mother.

I have a new start. My life has been slowly building up for me now. Life is hard, but my advice is: Don't give up, even if everyone turns their back on you. Everyone seems so mean, so ugly. It seems there's no point in living and you're never going to see light … You know what? There's always a light out there. You just have to find it.

I look at problems as a game. I believe God gives you problems to prepare you for life; to prepare you to grow up; to help you build a strong self-esteem; to be a strong person to fight this world. That's how I got through it. I kept saying to myself, "You either make it or you leave it. You either die with trying hard or you die with nothing." That's how I see it. If you don't try hard enough, you'll die regretting it. If you try, at least you—even if you don't make it, even if you're not the rich person you want to be—at least you tried. That's all that matters.

Life is about trying, it's not about what you want, it's not about what you wish. It's not about magic. Life is about trying, and about how you see life. If you think every day that life sucks and isn't worth living, you're not going to have a good life. When you wake up in the morning, make a goal for yourself or do something nice for someone.

I feel bad about myself sometimes. I will go for a walk and bring 50¢. If I see a homeless person, I'll give them 25¢. If I see another homeless person, I'll give them 25¢, or sit and talk to them. Or volunteer. Do anything to make yourself feel good about yourself. That's the way you should do it. Don't try to smoke cigarettes or weed again. Try to make yourself strong and try to make yourself look good, because people don't look at you as though you're cool, they look at you as though you're a stupid person who follows other people's rules.

If you get into crime and violence, it's not that easy to get out. Yeah, you see people driving sports cars, a whole bunch of people beating people up, holding guns … You know what? That's not what we're about. You want someone to boss you around and tell you to kill someone? Or do you want to ruin your life and spend the rest of it in jail? Or do you want to make money a good way? Work hard and earn your money; that way your money is always safe. If you get money a dirty way, the money never stays. That's my advice.

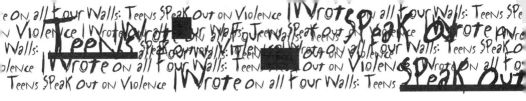

Don

Don drew attention to himself by fighting, intimidating those around him, and speaking out. He wanted to show off his superiority and control over others—while masking his own insecurities.

I was violent right from when I was a little kid. I would bully my younger brother and sister.

I was talking about this the other day with my brother and he told me how, as a young kid, he'd be afraid to go to sleep at night. I would often wait in his room, under his bed. He remembered one time lying in his bed with the lights off and all of a sudden I jumped out from under the bed and put a knife up to his throat. I was probably about eight at the time. He was four.

He'd tell my parents about stuff, but they had a lot of trouble disciplining me. One time they told me to go to my room and stay there with no dinner, so I threw a chair through my bedroom window. I just had a really bad temper if I got in trouble.

There was a period there when I just wanted to see how people would react if I did things that you normally wouldn't do. A lot of times I would send someone into a situation where I knew they were going to get in a lot of trouble. For instance, if I wanted to try something new that I was a little afraid to try myself, I'd get someone else to do it. I'd just completely harass them until they did it, like smoking, or making my own cigarette out of rolled-up paper and grass. I'd light it and tell someone else to smoke it or I'd beat the crap out of them.

My parents moved to a suburb when I was about 10 years

29

old. I was the oldest kid on the street and I was a fair-sized kid. I wasn't stupid, but I was always a little bit screwed-up. I wanted to see what would happen if I made this kid throw a brick through a window or something. He'd be like, "You can't throw a brick through the window," and I'd just smack the kid around until he did it. So he'd throw the brick through the window and I'd be long gone. Now I know what a cowardly thing I did, hiding in the bushes down the street.

I found out a little while ago that one of my friends, who my mom babysat when we were little, just dreaded me coming anywhere near him. I always hurt him in some way. He was always crying. Physical stuff aside, I think I combined it with making him afraid to do something for fear of physical consequences. I got my way by intimidating people.

I wasn't the toughest kid at school by any means. There are those kids who are just huge and could physically demolish people if they chose to. A lot of the things I did were in reaction to them. I remember we were playing road hockey and this big kid, Jerry, he just kept pounding me into the ground, and I couldn't do anything about it because he was twice my size. I was getting so mad at him. One time he came running up towards me and I knew I was going to go into the snowbank in two seconds, so I hit him in the head with my hockey stick before he got me. I don't know why I did it, I just knew I didn't want to get hit by this guy, so I just took him out. I don't know if I wanted to hurt him, but I do know I wanted to not go down in the snowbank again.

If anyone ever hurt me, it would embarrass me to the point that I would stew about it and get into a crazy rage about it. I would dwell on it for days until I found a way to get them back.

Things would embarrass me that wouldn't embarrass someone else. Somebody could say, "Nice shoes," in a bit of a snide tone and I'd lose my mind over it. Even if I didn't do anything at the time, later on I'd come up and smoke them from behind for no reason. They'd fall over and get hurt, all because they'd said something stupid to me a few days before.

I don't know why I did it. I was really insecure. I don't know if it was about being outsmarted. I always had to have the upper hand. I didn't want to feel I was below anyone, so if I couldn't find the words to defeat them, I'd do something to them later. I planned revenge.

I guess it's like a lesser version of one of those Columbine kids who just shoot everyone. Maybe it's like if you say something to someone like, "Ooh, look what he's wearing!" or "Why are you wearing a black trench coat again? You look retarded!" Certain people, I guess, have fragile minds and they can't handle anything like that and they stew about it. They just go away and think about what that guy said to them and how he embarrassed them. Next thing you know, that guy's on a death list.

In school, I always hung out with the popular kids. If they started on something, I would follow suit there too. I was the really mouthy one. I still am. I will still mouth off to random people if they do something I don't like or something that gets me in trouble. I embarrass my girlfriend all the time, still, to this day. Recently we saw some people get into a fender-bender and then they just parked in the middle of the road. The police aren't going to come to a fender-bender. I thought they should just pull over, exchange numbers, and deal with it—get out of the way. I pulled up beside them, rolled down my window, and let them have it.

On the weekend, I was in Ikea. A lady dropped something and it smashed. Everyone was quiet, but I started acting like it was a big deal, saying, "Ohhhhhhhhhhh!" and pointing at her. I don't know why I suddenly resorted back to something I would have done in public school. I just started laughing at her and pointing at her. My girlfriend and her mom were embarrassed.

Sometimes I do things where I don't recognize myself.

I started working in a factory when I just turned 14. There were a lot of students that came in on Saturday morning. The head student was the foreman. So it actually became a sort of Saturday morning high school. All these students would show up to clean and sometimes even run machines. We learned how to do things. The boss would come in in the mornings and check on us. After a while he trusted us to do it because we'd do a good job. Occasionally, though, we'd work really hard for the morning, then we'd have two hours to kill, to screw around.

There was this one guy whose name was Vince. He was a loser at his high school. He was a stereotype: glasses, socially retarded (he didn't know how to talk to people). He sounded stupid even though he wasn't stupid. I exploited every little problem we had with him. I'd bully the shit out of this kid all the time. Everyone else would do it too.

One Saturday at work this guy and I went after him, jumped him, and got his arms really quick. We were both way stronger than this kid. We taped him so he couldn't move. We taped his legs, threw him up against the pole, taped around his face so he couldn't see, with only his nose and mouth free, and left him there for about two and a half hours, and took off. We thought it was so funny.

We were originally gonna leave him there for a couple of seconds, but it turned into a battle of wills between me and the other guy to see who was going to cut him loose first. It became about me and the other guy. This poor fuckin' Vince just got caught in it.

Finally, we went and cut him loose. When he was free, he just ran out of the factory and he never came back. He never even called to quit or anything, so we never got in trouble for it. He just took off.

I used to get into fights, random ones. I'd pick fights with people. Especially at high school parties or dances.

There's a group mentality with teenage boys. If you're with all your buddies, you've gotta stick your chest out, kind of thing. When you hear people say that teenagers are idiots, you don't get it while you're a teenager. Now I look back and think, "Holy shit! I don't know what I was thinking!" Something was really wrong with the way I was thinking. What made a group of us want to prove ourselves like that? It wouldn't even necessarily be me who did the fighting any particular night, but I'd always be a part of it in some way. If one of my friends was involved, we were all involved.

I never stabbed anyone or anything, although I carried a knife. I never actually used it against anyone. I threatened people with it and they'd run away. I carried it more to impress than to actually hurt someone.

I remember going through the schoolyard and slashing bike tires and stuff. It wasn't a butcher knife or anything; it was a hunting knife. I carried a knife all through middle school and only stopped when I got into high school.

I was into doing bad things to the school building because you're supposed to hate school. I'd throw eggs at the school, throw rocks through windows, and other stupid stuff. It's pretty popular to throw rocks. Every weekend, every school in the city probably takes rocks through their windows.

The first time I hurt someone badly was when I got into a serious hockey fight when I was about 16. We started mask to mask. He was saying crazy stuff and he spat in my face. I just went crazy. I started tearing at him. I gave every ounce of aggression I had. I pulled his helmet right off his head.

Everyone was trying to break it up. I connected a perfect punch right into the guy's nose and blood squirted out into the air and I saw it. I saw the look on his face and then he just fell over. He was done. Then the refs pulled me away.

It really shook me up. At first I didn't want to play hockey any more. I got suspended for five weeks, but I played again after that.

I ended up getting into another fight about a year later. My nose got broken. It hurt for a long time. I had headaches all the time and I was black under my eyes. It was a really bad break. I thought, "This is what I did to that guy." That was when I really started thinking. I know that sounds like a stupid thing to say, but that was when I started thinking about consequences. I never had before. I started thinking, "Why am I hurting people? Why did I get hurt? Why did this happen?"

It suddenly seemed so stupid to me. Then I just sort of stopped wanting to hurt, stopped caring, started wanting to have more fun. It was a gradual thing, not like I had an epiphany or anything. It's like I grew out of it, almost.

I've been in fights since then, like at college, but they're different. I didn't want them to happen. I wasn't looking for a fight. One time in college, I was at a bar talking to a girl and a guy came up and tapped me on the shoulder, and when I turned, he punched me. Of course I got crazy mad and we started fighting. Afterwards, though, I felt much more shaken up about it than I would have when I was younger. I almost cried. I got all screwed up about it. I didn't want to fight.

I saw a fight about a month and a half ago where I work. The manager got punched in the face. I work in a beer store in a rough neighborhood. The guy got creamed. I broke it up and handled it fine, but after, I was really shaken up about it again. I don't know why I think differently about it now.

When someone's growing up, you have to be really careful because there are things I would have done when I was 14, like 10 years ago, that I wouldn't ever do now. I don't feel like I have to prove anything. If you look at all the violence in high schools, it's like they don't think about the consequences. I don't have any idea why they don't. I didn't either.

My parents knew, but they really didn't want to believe it. My mom wore rose-colored glasses. She would try to suppress me and she'd try to punish me like I was a two-year-old when I was a teenager, but it doesn't work. She'd tell me I couldn't play Nintendo for three days or something like that. I'd think, "I don't care. Fine." Or she'd say I had to stay in my room, and I'd say, "All right." There was a period of about a year, starting when I was about 14, when things were really bad.

She would try to smother me. She's still like that. It's just her nature. It's not her fault. She'd try to keep me in my room or she'd try to pretend it wasn't happening, that I wasn't doing stupid shit. She'd cry and try to get me to come in and hug her while she was crying. She'd turn it around, all crazy, guilt-based. She'd try to make me feel guilty to stop me from what I was doing.

I felt so guilty all the time, but it wouldn't stop me. I still feel the repercussions of guilt now. It made our relationship a little screwed-up, I think. We have a relationship based on guilt now.

When I was in high school, I smoked pot, did drugs, and drank all the time. My dad knew. He wouldn't let me come inside sometimes because he didn't want my mom to see me. He'd catch me in the driveway. He'd tell me to take a walk around the block and come home when I was sober. He was more aware of it than my mother was. He's been known to have a few himself.

I was so mean to my parents. They'd tell me I had to stop doing something and I'd say, "Shove it." Like every other teenager, you don't respect authority. You think your parents are repressing you.

I bet if you asked a lot of teenage boys why they did violent stuff, they'd say they don't know why. It's like an alpha-male kind of thing, I think. You just want to be powerful and you want to be in control. When, for instance, we were taping the guy up in the back room, we were so in control of that situation. We were that guy's boss. He couldn't do anything and we were completely in charge.

My parents gave me choices. They never told me I had to do this or that. That worked for someone like my sister, who is very able to focus on one thing and knows what she wants to do and knows how to sit down and do her homework. For someone like me, it didn't work. My parents were not strict at all. Even if I stayed out all night, they'd still let me in the house. They just didn't discipline us. Again, that worked with my sister but it didn't work so well with me. I did what I liked. The only thing I knew I liked doing was having fun. I couldn't focus. I think my parents tried, but it must be impossible trying to raise someone like me.

When you don't have a focus, it's hard to figure out what you want to do with your life. Even in high school, people put pressure on you to be good in school. You have to go to school, but you don't really know why. You don't understand at that point what school is good for, why you're doing things. You just go to class and learn all these things that you don't really feel like learning and you don't get why you're doing things. Some people know what they want to do when they're born. If you don't, when you're a teenager you are surrounded by confusion. All guys want to be the president of the company, but on a teenage scale the company is a bunch of idiots, and if you want to be the president of a bunch of idiots, you have to make sure no one picks on you. If anyone picks on you, you have to make them pay for it so no one else will pick on you and you stay in charge.

By college, I was drinking way too much. I actually had to go to the hospital because I drank too much hard liquor. I rotted away a lot of my stomach lining and couldn't eat because my stomach hurt most of the time and I was coughing up blood and stuff like that. I had to take medication.

I think it got that bad because I got a reputation early on that I liked to party really, really hard and I'd be a lot of fun. I liked the reputation. By fourth-year college, everybody thought I was crazy because I stopped going out, I stopped going to bars, I stopped doing everything. All I did was go to school and go home and sleep. I didn't want to do anything else. I just wanted to straighten up. I stopped doing drugs, I stopped drinking.

The girl I started dating had a lot to do with me cleaning up. She was the first girl I really, really cared about, so I cleaned up because I wanted to get together with her.

I have changed, but not in all respects. I have always wanted to get a reaction out of people, even when I was little, before I got totally violent. I always wanted to create a drama, out of boredom or something. If getting a reaction meant picking up a snowball and putting a rock into it and chucking it at a kid's head, I'd do it just to see what would happen.

As I got older, when I was in college, I was really starting to come out of it. I went through a really brutal time where I was trying to suppress my violence. I'd smash my own head against the wall to stop myself from letting violence out. I think that's too extreme. I don't think I'm a ticking time bomb or anything, but I need to find a happy medium—a balance.

I still think I'm probably not quite there yet, as far as being focused. I still have a lot of confusion about a lot of things, but the way it manifests itself is a lot more positive than it used to be.

I don't think you can just change. I think, when you decide to change, you go to the opposite extreme, which often is just as bad. You have to find somewhere in the middle. I still get mad, like everyone else. I still get sad, I still get happy, but it's more focused. I can stop myself from getting really mad and even apologize.

My parents told us a story the other day about coming upstairs and catching my brother trying to Krazy Glue my bedroom door shut while I was in there because he didn't want me to get out. He was just a little kid too.

My brother never became a bully. He's way taller than me and he's about 50 pounds heavier, with muscles and stuff now. No one would ever dream of messing with him. He was huge. He was always the gentle giant. He'd defend himself, he'd stand up for people and stuff, but he's a very peaceful guy.

When I was little, I'd kick the shit out of him and everyone would say, "He's going to be bigger than you, you'd better watch out!" By the time he was 16 and I was 20, we got along really well.

I try and figure it all out sometimes. There was a girl I was seeing in college who was completely convinced that I was out there to ruin my own life. She thought I was very self-destructive. She was a really, really intelligent girl. She was always analyzing everything, over-analyzing.

I wasn't really violent at that time, but I was mouthy and very hard on my body. I would work out really hard, but I'd still go out and get "killed," so I was always really hard on myself physically. Maybe I was, as she said, self-destructive, but it's such a weird thing to think. I don't want to die or anything, so when I consider it I have to say no, but when I look back at the way I acted, why did I do certain things if that wasn't the case? I have no explanation.

I don't know what kind of help I needed. I think I just needed some direction. No one ever gave me any of that. I don't know if anyone *could* have given me any. How do you put someone on a path to becoming something? I think one of the reasons is that, when you're younger, there's so much pressure on you to *become* something, but you already are something *then*. People forget that. Everyone always talks about the future and what they're going to do and what they're going to be, but when you're that young, you don't think about that. You just wonder why you should do this or that. You don't think about the future, you just kind of *do* stuff. There really wasn't anyone to tell me not to do it.

I don't think I was an anomaly. I think everything's just separated into a chain of random violence and emotional violence and stuff. I was just lucky that I was closer to the top— not at the top but close—because I didn't get abused by other bullies as much. I was like someone that maybe *I* would have picked on.

I wish I had more regrets than I do. I feel guilty about the fact that I don't feel that guilty, if that makes sense. When I look back, I don't think I ruined anyone's life or anything. I just got mean sometimes and I don't really have an explanation for it. If I tried to apologize to someone and say, "Hey, I'm sorry I made your life hell for the first year of college," I *couldn't* apologize for it because I still don't even know why I did it. It would be like, "Sorry, there, for what it's worth."

I hated to be the victim. If I ever was, I would consider it a loss and I'd try to work a rematch in, where I knew I was going to win. I couldn't have handled knowing there was some guy out there who had beat me, even if he'd only pushed me down a hill or told me he didn't like my hat in front of girls or something.

I think with some guys it gets magnified. It's competitive. Wanting to win is a good thing. If you're a bully and you beat up another kid, somewhere in your mind maybe you feel shitty about something else. Maybe the big fat kid who decides to beat the hell out of a smaller kid because someone has been calling him fat all his life—when he beats up the other kid, he wins that one. It's his way of saying, "I can win something too, you know! I don't care if you're skinny."

If someone embarrassed me, I'd have to embarrass them back. I have to win. I probably inherited that from my dad. He likes to win. Even in sports and stuff, anything less than 100 percent was unacceptable. I'd get the lecture in the car on the way home from hockey about how lame I'd played after a game. I know it wasn't just me that happened to; lots of kids heard that from their dads. So at the next game I'd really go after someone. How do you stop that cycle?

I think I've always just been really sensitive to criticism, ever since I was a little kid. I still am. I take it better than I did before. Even if someone gave me a whole list of compliments, even one little, tiny criticism would stick with me. I'd confront them about the criticism and wouldn't be able to hear anything else. I'd just stick to that one negative thing and wouldn't be able to stop thinking about it. It's like constant pressure. That's something I am still learning to deal with.

I think I do too much thinking now. I overcompensate. I can't sleep. I'm so different from how I used to be, yet I'm not different. I don't know. It's weird. I guess I am still trying to find the balance.

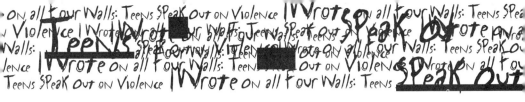

Debbie

Debbie's relationship with an abusive boyfriend began during her college days.

I was in my second year of college when I met John. I was 19; he was six months younger. We met through a mutual friend I knew from high school whom John was going to college with.

John's a very good-looking guy. The first time I met him, he had the kind of attitude I find attractive. He was a bit arrogant. Maybe arrogance isn't a good word, but rather, confident in himself. He was tall and well built, with broad shoulders, which I found very attractive. He was funny, and thought I was attractive.

Looking back, I'd say there were no warning signs that he could be violent. Not the first time we met, not until we were officially dating.

He had a girlfriend when we first met, and I was kind of the "other woman" in the beginning. We continued to see each other until he broke up with his girlfriend, then we carried on dating. We met in March. Ten months later, he moved into my apartment.

The first significant incident occurred before then, when he used to visit on weekends. I can't pinpoint the exact time, but I know it was before he was living with me—about seven months into the relationship.

We argued—I can't remember what about. We used to argue a lot. He had a very short fuse and little things would set him off. He would get upset if I wanted to go somewhere and he wanted to spend time with me. If I wanted to do something like go shopping with a friend or do something without him, it would really upset him because he wanted to spend time with me. That was always his reason: "I want to spend time with you." So I felt guilty a lot.

But really, anything could set him off. He was very unpredictable. Sometimes when we were driving together and I did something he didn't feel was right, for example. If we stopped at a stop sign at the same time as another car and I gave the other car the right-of-way, he would think it was my right-of-way, and that would erupt into a big argument. It really could be anything.

I can remember the first violent incident. We were arguing in my apartment. After the argument had calmed down a bit, he asked me whether I thought he was abusive. I remember thinking about the question; there was a pause between his question and my answer because I didn't know what to say to make the argument end. I thought it would be pretty safe if I answered no, but I believed the true answer was yes, he was abusive. Then I thought that maybe *he* thought he was abusive, and maybe he wanted to deal with it, so I said yes.

He blew up! He pushed me down on the bed, pinned my hands above my head and got really close to my face with our noses almost touching (which is something he did a lot), and yelled at me. Often when he screamed and yelled I could feel the spit from his words on my face.

I remember him telling me that I didn't know what abuse was, and that he had never hit me. He didn't pin me down for long. He knew it was wrong. But then he said he was leaving, just for the night. He was going to go to a friend's.

I didn't want him to leave. I tried to tell him that I didn't mean it, that he wasn't abusive. Then he pushed me up against a wall. He's six feet and I'm five feet; he weighs 200 pounds and I'm 115 pounds, so it was not hard for him to do. He wasn't *extremely* violent, it didn't hurt, but it was forceful. And we weren't far away from the wall, maybe a foot. It was just so he had some control and he could make me listen, which was a big thing with him.

He did end up leaving that night, but before he left he told me very calmly and nicely that he loved me and he was only leaving for the night. After he left, I sobbed for hours. My roommate woke up. She had heard the argument. We chain-smoked and made fried egg sandwiches. I cried, and she tried to make me feel better.

I wished I hadn't said that I thought he was abusive. I knew when it came out of my mouth that it wasn't the smart thing to say in terms of making the argument end, which is what my goal was. That was always my goal with him: how can I put this fire out? I shouldn't have said it. Even now, I can still say I shouldn't have said it because it didn't do me any good.

Even before this happened, I thought he was abusive. He yelled and swore a lot, and that's stuff that I'm not used to. Growing up, we didn't do that in my family. It just wasn't anything that I was used to. The boyfriend I had previous to him was the polar opposite. He was incredibly sweet, treated me like a queen, and never, ever, yelled at me, ever. He never touched me in a negative way. This was nothing I was used to.

I felt like crap that night, but I kept going, I guess because I knew his family, his background. John's father, when they lived in Ireland, shot people and blew things up for a living. When they moved to Canada, he became a police officer. John has scars on his stomach from when his father burned him with cigarettes. They're not like that now, they've changed a lot, but he was abused as a child.

His family, even to this day, settle things by yelling at each other and screaming and swearing. John would tell me stories about how they would punch each other. His parents would punch the kids. The two boys, once they got older, would punch each other back and forth. They were very physical. Again, not something I was brought up with. My brothers never fought with kids at school or with each other. It just wasn't something that I thought was acceptable or necessary in life. John's view was that all boys fight, and I didn't understand that. I didn't believe that some fights couldn't be avoided. So we differed in a lot of ways.

The thing with John's abuse was that he never did exactly the same thing twice. The other thing is, unlike a lot of abusive couples who have a honeymoon period, we never had that after an incident. I would often get an apology, but never a lot of sweetness or presents.

Once, we had an argument (I can't remember what it was about because it was usually really insignificant) and I left the apartment to go downstairs where a friend lived, which is something he really hated me to do. He never, ever, let me leave during an argument. *He* could leave. He always left—slammed the door, took off in the car, whatever—but he would never let me leave. He would physically block me from leaving.

Somehow, though, I got out of the apartment that night and went down the stairwell. He came to the stairwell (this was in the middle of the night) and he yelled obscenities at me at the top of his lungs. I wrote down the names he called me in my journal because for some reason I decided I was going to keep track of them, but he never called me any names after that, which is why I'm saying he seldom did the same thing twice.

I often ask myself now why I stayed with him. I really cared about him a lot and thought things could change. I understood how he was brought up, thought we really loved each other and could work through it. We even started to see a therapist at the college. But he always thought she was on my side and that she wasn't fair, that she was biased. So we only had three sessions with her.

The one thing I remember from those sessions was the issue of laundry. I had problems with him tossing his clothes all over the bedroom and not using the laundry hamper that was right there. So the therapist helped us decide that we were going to get another laundry basket, as though two baskets would help the problem. It was so stupid; it didn't help at all.

We never got into any details with the therapist because I was so afraid to talk about it, afraid that he would leave me, and I didn't want that, that's why I stuck through it. And things weren't always horrible. They really weren't. After the breakup, that was the main thing I wanted people to understand. He wasn't horrible and it wasn't horrible every minute. We had a lot of good times, but the horrible stuff really outweighed the good stuff.

I gradually began to realize that things weren't going to change.

Another big thing with him (and this did happen multiple times) was when we'd be in an argument, I would be really upset and he'd say, "Well, if you think you're so abused, if you think I'm so mean to you, why don't you call someone?" Then he'd pick up the phone and either dial my parents' number, dial his parents' number, or dial 911, and I would promptly run over to the wall and unhook the phone, or hang up the phone if I could. He would also dial it then throw the phone at me so that I would have to talk. The other thing he'd do was get the phone book and throw the phone book at me and tell me to call a woman's shelter or an abuse hotline. Or he'd open it up and put it right in my face and say, "Call *this* number, call *them* if you think you're so abused."

I wouldn't. I never wanted to talk to my parents or his parents about it. Not then.

I'm not extremely educated on the topic of abuse, but I had learned about it from high school as well as college. Part of me thinks that he must have known that something was wrong, but another part of me says he must have absolutely believed he wasn't doing anything wrong, because if I actually had called, he thought they'd tell me I was being stupid. That's exactly what he said, that if I called, they'd tell me that I was being ridiculous, that I wasn't being abused, that I was oversensitive and emotional.

Part of the reason I didn't call was because I didn't know what would happen if I did. Would they come and take him away? Would they charge him? I never wished any ill on him at all. I still don't. I would never press charges against him for anything. I didn't want the police to do that. I wanted him to get help. I never would have called them, and he probably knew that, so it was a safe thing for him to do.

In terms of physical violence, other than pushing me against the bed and the wall, he never really did anything else against me, but he often would be physical with things, objects, property. In our first apartment he ripped the shower curtain down once and punched a hole in our bedroom door, which I patched. In one of our Hamilton apartments he punched a hole in the living-room wall, which I patched and painted because we were subletting. The bedroom door was off its hinges from him slamming it and opening it, slamming it and opening it multiple times. In our other Hamilton apartment there was a hole in the closet door and a hole in our bedroom door.

He would just punch and his hand would go right through. Often he had cuts on his hands from punching walls, doors, or furniture. He used to throw things. He threw an alarm clock across the room and it broke. Candle holders shattered. Once he ripped the shirt I was wearing off me. It was his shirt and I was wearing it. He ripped it off, then ripped the shirt he was wearing off himself to show me that it wasn't bad if he did it to himself too.

It freaked me out when he got like that. I'm not used to that kind of behavior. I used to say, "What are you doing? I mean, rather the walls than me, but my God, do you have no self-control?" It was really scary. Sometimes I would get so scared I would cower in a corner. He thought I was being ridiculous, but what else are you going to do but back up into a corner to get away from the rage? That would piss him off even more. He'd say, "Oh my God! You're *scared* of me. Why are you scared of me?" Then he'd get really intimidating. There was nothing I could do, I would basically be in shock. My eyes would be wide, just watching him do this. I'd say, "John, calm down. Calm … breathe …" Mostly I just stayed quiet and let him do what he had to do because I learned, throughout the three years, just to shut up. Shut up, be still, don't cry, don't say anything, don't be calm and use a calm voice—don't do that, it pisses him off. Don't do *anything*. But then that pissed him off too. When he got like that, there was nothing I could do. Nothing was right. Nothing.

We talked about it sometimes. Sometimes, when he was in a good mood or a sexual mood, I would try to talk to him and tell him how concerned I was about his behavior. I said, "Right now I think you're really stressed out. I think you have a lot going on in your life right now, but I don't want you to take it out on me." I tried to be very loving and would kiss him on the neck while

I was saying this to him so that he knew I wasn't trying to be confrontational. He would say, "I know. I'm really stressed out right now. I don't want to talk about it." That was his signature: I don't want to talk about it. He always chalked it up to his job and said he was really stressed out about his job. That I understood. He worked in a group home for kids in trouble with the law. It's all very ironic. He always wanted to talk about his feelings. And when he wanted to, I had to shut up and listen. I could never talk to him about how I felt. Never.

He did have a very stressful job; I understand that completely. These kids are violent. He went through a lot. The problem is, he took it home. The other thing is, he had coverage for therapy and he never took advantage of it. I used to tell him, "Hey, you have coverage now. Why don't you go and talk to somebody about the stresses at work?" He didn't. He wouldn't. So I think these kids got the best of him and I got the worst of him. But even before he had this job, he was like this. So I think to a certain extent he got worse with the stresses. Once he got a promotion, when he was really deep into the job full-time, it did, to a certain extent, escalate. But it was always there.

My family took a really long time to warm up to John. They didn't know any of the bad stuff. I never talked to anybody about it, especially my family. They were very cautious of him to begin with. The second time they ever met him was the first year we were dating, when he came home with me for Thanksgiving. We went downtown to a bar with another couple and we got into a cab to go home. This other group of people thought it was their cab, and a fight broke out. John broke his hand in two places punching someone and spent the night in the hospital getting his hand all fixed up. So my parents were very concerned about that and his tendency towards violence.

That was pretty hard on my family. The brother I'm closest

to didn't like John at all for a very long time because of the way we had started dating, with John already having a girlfriend and me being the other woman. He felt it wasn't secure. When we got engaged, everybody warmed up. My brothers thought, OK, this must be serious then, that I obviously really cared about him, and they started to be OK. My mom never liked John as much as she had liked my previous boyfriend, who was very hard to top.

So my family always said they thought I was the best thing that ever happened to John when we were dating. When we were engaged, they said that, that I had helped him in life so much. But they never knew what was going on; they thought we were very happy. But I always felt tension between them and John. John bitched about my family a lot, which was very hard for me. We'd spend a weekend at the cottage with them and on the drive home, for three hours, that's all I would hear, him bitching about my family.

I never did that about his family. There were things about his family I didn't like, and that annoyed me, but I never shared that with him because it wasn't fair. I concentrated on the good things about his family because there were definitely things I liked, and we would talk about that. But I would never bitch about his family because I think that's such a sensitive issue for people. So, there was definitely tension. He thought my mom thought that he was stupid. He thought my dad never listened to him.

John was basically very insecure. In the beginning I was attracted to his confidence. Turns out he's very insecure about himself. He thought everybody thought he was stupid. That was a big thing with him. And he's not stupid. I think he has a learning disability, but he's not stupid.

About a month before I left him, he had been out with some friends at a bar, where they had a few drinks. He had the car and came to pick me up from work. When I got into the car, he said I should drive. I asked why and he said because he'd just had a few beers. I said, "But you just drove from the bar to pick me up!" Plus, it was *my* car—well, my parents' car. So I got into the driver's seat and on the way home, which was about a three-minute drive, I said, "John, you could have called me from the bar, we could have arranged something. I don't want you to drive after drinking, and clearly you don't think you're good enough to drive, so why did you?" And he said, "I'm not good enough to drive with *you* in the car." I said, "What the hell difference does it make?" At this point we were already engaged and I said, "You're going to be the father of my children, and even if you're alone in the car, you're the father of my children and I don't want you to die. I understand you don't want to kill *me* if you're driving drunk, but you're important too."

We got home to the apartment and it blew up. I had had a cousin who was under the influence, drove a car into a tree, and died, so it was a very sensitive issue. John said, "I'm not Buddy! I'm not your stupid 15-year-old cousin!" I started crying and he said, "Why are you crying, no one's here who can hear you. There's no one here to impress."

Crying was the worst thing I could do, it made him so angry. That's why I learned not to cry most of the time. He thought I did it for attention, to make people feel sorry for me, to make him feel bad. At one point he even said he wouldn't yell if I wouldn't cry. That didn't happen even after I stopped crying; the yelling continued throughout the relationship.

So, this time again, he was screaming so close to my face. The redness of his face is still so vivid, and the spit on my face. He knocked over a fan. Then he started to close all the windows so we couldn't be heard. Then there was a knock at the door. I sneaked into the bedroom and he went to get the door. I heard him say, "Come in, sir." And I thought, here we go. I knew it was the police.

I stood in the hallway and could hear him talking. He invited the two police officers in. One took me to the end of the hallway and the other took John into the living room. They talked to us separately. The one guy asked me what we were arguing about, but I didn't tell him John was driving under the influence. I said we were having an argument and that John has a bad temper and a very booming voice, which is true. I didn't lie about anything. They said the neighbors called and were concerned, so they had to come and check it out. I said thanks and told him we were both really stressed out right now, that we both have really high-stress jobs, and that was it. They left. Nothing ever happened. The police officer saw that the fan was knocked down and asked if he pushed it over. I said no, that he'd knocked into it, which wasn't true. So I guess I did lie.

After that, I felt that I was trailer trash, which is a horrible phrase, I know. I felt like it was a life I didn't want to be living, where the police were called, where my fiancé yelled at me so loudly that the neighbors could hear. The neighbors had told the police that this wasn't the first time they could hear yelling from our apartment.

I cried that night for a really long time and decided it wasn't how I wanted to live. I finally realized that nothing was going to change because John wasn't willing to change. He had promised me many times to go to anger management, but it never happened. I don't think he thought that anything he did was wrong. He told me everybody yelled, that all couples do this, that we wouldn't fight so much if we weren't so in love.

I asked him if he was like this with his old girlfriend, who was a high school girlfriend. They never lived together or anything. He said no, but that he didn't love her like he loved me.

I know now it wasn't me; it's really who he is. It's going to be the same way with the next girl he lives with, or marries. It's pretty tough. He was very anxious to get married, very anxious to have kids. It's scary to think of him as a father.

During the last month together I found myself daydreaming about a life without him. I found myself falling asleep at night thinking about other people I could date. Not anyone in particular, just a life without John. I started to get very sleepless, nauseous, anxious, and overall just feeling like this was not right. And I think I always knew that it wasn't right from the day he proposed—well, from the day we bought the ring. I didn't want to buy it.

My mom saw John once on a really bad day and asked me what was going on. I said, "He's in a bad mood. Days like this I just hate." She said his moods sometimes reminded her a bit of my dad's. They never saw any of the bad stuff, they only saw this moodiness, and my dad can be moody. She said, "Debbie, I never saw any of this before I married your dad. You kind of have a chance." That's all she said. It kind of resonated in me, and I thought, yeah, I don't have to live with this for the rest of my life; I'm only engaged, I'm not married.

During that last month I didn't want to plan my wedding. My whole life I had looked forward to getting married, and I still do. I dreamed about the white dress and the big day like most girls, but I didn't want to plan this wedding. I would go to friends' houses with bridal magazines and my wedding planner, with the full intention of starting this, then I'd say, "Let's do something else." I didn't want to do it.

My sex drive was extremely low. John was a very sexual person. He had a very high sex drive and thought his needs should be fulfilled whenever they were there, which was all the time, and I just wasn't into that. But I am a sexual person. In past relationships I've had a high sex drive and been fine, but I didn't want any part of it. He thought I didn't love him, he thought I wasn't attracted to him any more. He's a very attractive man, in my mind. I did love him, so I finally said I was going to go to the doctor. The doctor put me on steroid pills and steroid cream. I took them for two days, then I said, "I'm not doing this. This is bad for my body." So I stopped.

John went to work overnight one night, and as soon as he left at six o'clock, I called my mom. I said, "Mom, I'm scared." She asked, "What's going on?" I said, "I don't know if I should talk to you about this. Can you try to remain non-judgmental and impartial? I just need to talk about it." She asked, "What's going on?" "I think I want to leave John," I told her. She kind of went, "Oh. OK. Why?" I said, "I don't know. I just don't think I can do this any more. I don't want to marry him." We talked about it for an hour, and I said to her, "I just can't … I don't know what to do." She said, "I've talked to you for an hour, you know what to do. I think you're just too scared right now." And I said, "Yeah." It was a Thursday night, and she said, "Come to the cottage this weekend and we'll talk about it with your father. Can you do that?" I said, "Yeah, I'll just tell John I'm homesick and I want to go to the cottage for the weekend." I said, "I don't know how that's going to go over, but I'll try it."

Then I called a couple of friends and talked to them. They assured me that this was an OK decision, that I could do this. I ended up calling my mom back and saying, "I'm going to do this." It was decided that I was going to go to the cottage on Friday morning. John was going to drop me off at work with my suitcases and I was going to take the bus to Kingston. I was going to quit my job that day. On Monday we were going to come back and move me out. Somehow, that got decided Thursday night.

So I called John at work and said, "If it's OK with you, I'm going to go to the cottage this weekend because I'm feeling homesick and a bit down." He said it was fine because I'd caught him in a good mood. He didn't have any problem with that. That night he was working the night shift. I couldn't sleep. I woke up the next morning and got ready for work. He came home from work, had two coffees—and I went to the bathroom and threw up. I was so nervous. My body was a mess. He knocked on the bathroom door and said, "Do you want me to call work and tell them you're sick?" I said, "No, I'm fine." I kept throwing up. I was heaving. I had nothing in my stomach, but I was so nauseous.

John drove me to work and dropped me off. I said, "I love you," and I kissed him goodbye. It was the last time I saw him, but it wasn't intended that that would be the last time I would see him. It was still on my mind that on Monday I was going to tell him I was leaving him.

Over the weekend, I talked to my parents. I told my parents a lot of the negative stuff that had happened. They were very concerned for my safety. I talked to my cousin, the lawyer, and asked him what I needed to do to make sure that this was legal, that whatever I took was legal. He kind of convinced me that I shouldn't talk to John, that I should leave a note and just leave, because I knew John was working all day on Monday.

I did quit my job on the Friday morning, and told my boss why.

So we drove to Hamilton on the Monday morning. I stopped in at the rental place that we rented the apartment from and told them I was leaving. I told them I wouldn't be responsible for any damages to the apartment. I was afraid John was going to wreck the place when he found out I was gone and I didn't want to be responsible for that. They said all they could do was draft a letter to John asking him to let me out of the lease early, because both of our names were on the lease. I said that was fine, that I'd leave that with my note to him. I had drafted a letter to him, which I rewrote a couple of times.

Dear John,

By the time you read this, I will be gone. Believe me when I say that I do not mean to hurt you, but I have to do what is best for me. I believe that this is what is best for both of us. I have decided to write this letter because I feel that if I tried to talk to you face to face, it would simply erupt into an argument.

I have realized that I no longer know myself and that this relationship is not really working for either of us. I think we have been taking each other for granted and are not fulfilling each other's needs. Neither of us is truly happy, and I am not ready to get married with the way things are.

I cannot live with your unpredictable anger, or the yelling, or the property damage. I feel that I have given these things sufficient time to change, but they have not. And so, I need to change.

I know this will likely come as a great shock to you. And I am sorry for that. I have been trying to discuss my concerns with you for some time now, but you never want to talk about our relationship or my feelings. At this point, I feel I have no option but to end the relationship for now. Perhaps someday things will change, but for now I think we need to be apart.

I know this is hard for you to understand, but I do love you, John. I just don't think we are making good partners for each other right now. This is the hardest thing I have ever had to do, and the thought of hurting you breaks my heart. I wouldn't do this if I didn't think it was the best thing for both of us in the long term. I know you will be OK and find your life without me. I think you will be happier without me ... eventually. I feel like all I bring you is anger. And so this is the end for now. I hope we can remain friends. I will always hold a special place in my heart for you and I hope you will do the same.

My parents and I got to the apartment and packed frantically. John called me several times on my cellphone during this packing and he said, "Where are you?" I said, "I'm at the apartment with my parents." He said, "What are your parents doing there?" because I was supposed to have taken the bus. I said, "Well, we have to do some shopping. We're going to the mall." He was so mad at me, yelling at me. I said I had to go.

He called me back and in this very calm, quiet voice said to me, "Debbie, if you don't change your attitude, there is going to be World War III when I get home." He said it in a voice that I'd never heard him use before, ever. It was very monotone … it's so hard to even describe, like the scariest voice ever. I said, "OK," and hung up. I said to my parents, "We have to go. Now." I was afraid that he was going to come home.

We basically just booted it out of there. I left my note on the kitchen table along with a note from the rental agency, turned my keys in to the landlord, left my cat, and that was pretty much it.

We had a savings account with both our names on it. I went to the bank and took half the money. I put half the money into his account and closed the joint account. I did everything fairly—more than fair, in my estimation.

The other thing is, I kept the ring because we had about $3,000 of mutual debt on credit cards, most of it his. He will dispute until the end, but it was in my name, so the debt's all mine now, so I needed the ring, which is worth $5,000. It's still on sale. I'm still hoping for it to sell so I can pay off the credit cards.

The night I left, I turned my cellphone off. John left a message, though. It was the most horrid thing I'd ever heard in my entire life; I've never listened to anything harder. John left a message, sobbing like I've never heard him sob before, and he has cried in our relationship. He said, "Debbie, why have you done this? Where are you? Come back, please come back. I love you. I can change." I was really scared for him. My dad called his mom and said, "We're with Debbie. She's really concerned about John right now. We don't know if you know what's happened, but he left a message and we're scared for him." She said she knew, and that John's dad was on his way to see him. She wanted to get into it with my dad, but my dad said he wouldn't talk about it with her and got off the phone. I felt better knowing that his dad was going to be there because I was really scared that John was going to hurt himself.

I haven't seen him since. He called me once and he basically just swore at me for five minutes. When I asked why he was swearing at me, he said it was because I screwed him out of so much money. I said, "No, I haven't." I got off the phone and he e-mailed me and apologized for that, said it was inappropriate and that he was sorry. He still maintains that I've screwed him out of money, which I haven't. I don't want any contact with him. I want to put that away.

Now I am living with my parents. I was always very homesick for my family when I was away, so it's really nice to be close to them. I'm much freer to do what I want with my life, which is an incredible feeling. I'm working as an interior design consultant right now, which has always been a passion of mine. One day I was standing at work and I thought, Look at me! I'm not with John any more. I can go and date, I can do this, I can do that. I can take off tomorrow and do anything I want. I don't have to call him and tell him I'm going to be late, I don't have to argue. It's just like this gigantic weight is gone—like I've dropped two pant sizes.

I exercise. I have girlfriends. I had girlfriends before, but not the closeness that I have now. I have missed out. I read so much now. I've read 45 novels in the past six months, which is something I loved to do growing up. In high school I read fiction, which is something I never did when I was with John. I am obsessed with reading now; I do it all the time. I watch much less TV, which is good. The biggest thing is the girlfriends—the support.

I haven't dated since I left him. I'm ready to start dating. It's the sense of freedom and that I have control over my life. I listen to other people talking about their relationships and I'm like, what? It can be like that? I have a friend who is engaged and they are so funny. Things that John would scream at me for, her fiancé giggles: "Oh, you forgot to call me last night, eh?" And it's funny. John would have flipped out if I hadn't called him for a night. Things can be better.

Sometimes I get a little sad that I'm getting up there in my 20s—well, I'm almost 24— and I'm not attached. I want to have children, that's very important to me, but I'm very optimistic that there's someone out there who's going to love me better. I have been loved better, before John, and I'm positive that I can be loved better after John. I'm really looking forward to it. I want it to happen soon.

I never once doubted my decision. I get sad sometimes and miss him. I do miss him. I dream about him more often than I want to, but I've never once doubted that I made the right decision. I feel I have a chance at being really happy.

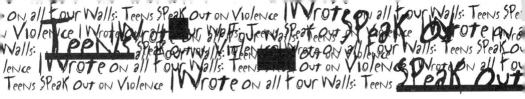

Janice

Janice's problems with bullying began at 14 when she started high school.

I am 16 now and I was 14 when the violence started. I was in a group at school and they seemed like really nice people. But everybody kind of changes when they get into high school. We were in Grade 9. People who seem nice will suddenly turn mean. Popularity rules over everybody. So I was in a group and they changed. I realized that I didn't want to go where they were going.

They started flunking, doing drugs, stuff like that. They were threatening people, yelling at people, shoving people in the halls. I decided that wasn't the best group for me to be with. So I found this other little quiet group of about 10 people. They were cool and really nice.

The group I dropped out of gave me a hard time, I guess because they thought I felt I was too good for them by not wanting to be part of what they were doing. They threatened me. I had a couple of incidents where people would hack into my e-mail account and e-mail my messages to other people. And they would send threatening messages like "Watch your back." I actually had one girl, Sara, threaten my life on the Internet. When we were talking on MSN Hotmail, she started yelling at me. I yelled back that she should just go away, that I didn't want to talk to her. She told me to shut up and said she was going to kill me.

I told my mom, but she really couldn't do anything about it because MSN Hotmail doesn't save your message history, so I didn't have a record of it. But a couple of my friends had been added to the Internet group. Sara thought it was cool when she threatened to kill me, but she didn't realize that some of the other group members were still friends with me. So I went to the principal's office the next day. He didn't do anything. He said we didn't have any real proof so he couldn't write it up, but he said, "We know she's threatened other people's lives, so we'll keep an eye on her."

I asked him what good it would do to keep an eye on her; they couldn't keep eyes on her all the time. I said I knew she was probably just being stupid, but what if I got hurt and he'd be to blame? I said, "It's your job on the line." He still didn't do anything.

Things like this aren't really dealt with properly in school society because of how bad things are getting. They can't go around suspending everybody for calling a person a dweeb or a jerk or something.

That same year, a little after I dropped out of that group, I was still friends with a few individual members. There was another girl, Victoria, who thought that her boyfriend was cheating on her with me. There were these rumors that I had done stuff with him in science class! Everyone had to realize that there was nothing to it. She said she wanted to fight me. She set a date for the following Wednesday.

I told my mom about the fight and then we told my dad. I didn't really get a reaction from him, but my mom was worried, so she decided to call the school. She was going to go in with me, but a lot of people at that school knew my mom because my brother had been in football, so we decided my sister Caroline would come in with me instead.

On the day the fight was going to happen, Caroline went to school with me. We went into the office after announcements and confronted the vice-principal. He said he'd have extra staff on duty at lunchtime and thanked us for making him aware of it. That made me feel better. I wasn't really scared, but I was a bit shaken up.

My family had me calmed down before I went to school, but as soon as I got there, I mean, I was by myself, right? So I was quite worried. Victoria wasn't a person you wanted to mess with, really. She was tough even though she was small. So I felt I had two options: I could fight her or I could go to the vice-principal and tell him what was going on and hope that he'd help me. But he didn't really help. Sure, there were two extra people on staff in the cafeteria. One person came into the cafeteria to talk to me. It was one of her friends who was also a friend of mine. She said, "You know what, she just wants to talk to you. I'll make sure she doesn't lay a hand on you." When it came to it, I actually didn't believe her, but she did make sure that Victoria didn't lay a hand on me. If it weren't for some of her friends that were friends with me too, I think I would have been hospitalized. You don't just fight one person any more, you fight that person and all their friends.

Victoria got me into the hall while there was no one there. All of a sudden, people started walking by and everybody knew there was supposed to be a fight. So people crowded all around me and Victoria in a big circle. Then the circle just started walking outside and I stopped, but people shoved me, so I had no option, I just had to keep on walking. We walked by a couple of teachers. A teacher stopped us the first time and told us to go to the cafeteria, but Victoria's friend came back and caught me before I got to the cafeteria. The group surrounded me again and I was forced outside.

This was Grade 9, my first year, so I was pretty frightened. I wasn't going to step up to people who were in Grade 10. Most of them were in Grade 10 and 11, some even in Grade 12.

So we walked outside and Victoria started yelling at me, "How could you do this? And why do you deny it? We know it's true!" Her boyfriend, Guy, was there and he was denying it too, but she was like, "I know it's true! Why don't you just tell us!"

I said to her, "I don't know you. I have no reason to do this to you. I have no reason to talk to you, to look at you, to smile at you. Why would I do that? You haven't given me a reason. I don't mean to sound full of myself, but I have a lot of guys that like me. Why would I go for a guy that already has a girlfriend?"

I did like this guy. We were good friends, but we never did anything. But she just didn't agree with me. So she was yelling at me outside. I don't know how long it went on for, maybe 10 minutes. They were all just standing there. We were in the smoke pit and everybody was just standing around watching and smoking.

I was actually feeling pretty calm because I had a friend, Justin, there. He's about six feet tall, between 250 and 280 pounds. He stood behind me the whole time, but I was still worried. He told me, "Even if they're girls, if one of them lays a hand on you, Janice, I'm there for you. I've got your back, don't worry about it."

So I was feeling pretty calm at the time, pretty good, because her friends were stepping up to her. One of her friends said, "You've made your point, Victoria. That's enough. Just stop." Then it was all over in a flash. She said, "Fine. Whatever." And she walked away.

So when the principal came out after it was all over, I looked at him and said, "You're worthless." He didn't like me for saying it, but he was. He did nothing. The staff—where were they? It doesn't take someone 10 minutes to get from point A to point B in a small school to tell them there was going to be a fight. I thought it was stupid. We were all called down to the office. Victoria was given an in-school suspension for about two days, which made it even worse because she was still in the school.

Victoria wasn't allowed to go near me, but her friends could. She had to sit in the office and do her work. She couldn't leave the office and had a different lunchtime than everyone else. But she could still go to the washroom, and there was still before and after school, so I still saw her.

Guy and Victoria eventually ended up breaking up. I talked to one of Victoria's friends. I was pretty honest with her. I said, "You know what? It didn't happen. I like the guy, I'll admit it, but it didn't happen. I wouldn't think about it. He's got a girl-friend. That's wrong. That's morally wrong."

The way I can figure it, it's pretty much all about popularity. One person has to be the tough person, one person has to be the weak person, and those two have to fight. I think she actually realized that she wasn't the tough person and she backed down.

That was pretty much the end of that. The principal didn't do anything about it, and as soon as people stopped talking about it, that was it.

My parents were very disappointed by the way the school handled the fight. They didn't feel that school was the best place for me. So I started being home-schooled—well, getting my work at home from school. But fights don't just happen at school.

One of my old friends, Jane, had run away from home and was living with one of the guys I was looking to go out with. She was living with Simon, his dad, and sister. This guy had asked me what she was like and stuff. He said, "My sister is missing clothes, she's missing jewelry. Do you think she did it?"

Simon's dad was getting pretty fed up because Jane wasn't holding her own around the house. She wasn't doing anything. She was rude to the sister, was rude to him. She was on the phone 24/7, didn't go to school any more, didn't have a job, and couldn't financially support herself. Simon was doing it all. He was a nice guy.

So I told him the truth about her: that I'd found things missing and then seen them in her room, that I didn't really trust her very much, but that when it came down to it she had usually been there for me and was a nice person, but I wouldn't suggest living with her. I suggested that he find her another place to live.

From that, she got the idea I told him to kick her out because I didn't want her there any more. She wanted to fight me. We've known each other for six years and she's put my life through hell, but I always forgive her. Jocelyn, a friend who was there, asked, "Are you honestly going to fight her?" I said, "If she hits me, I'm going to defend myself. I'm not going to stand there and let her hit me."

We were at the mall at the time, so we went outside. I turned to Jane and said, "If you want to hit me, hit me. It's pointless, because I didn't do anything, but if, for whatever reason, you're going to hit me when I turn my back, why don't you do it while I'm facing you?"

Jocelyn told her what I'd said about hitting her back if she hit me, so she walked away. That's the only reason she walked away—because she knew I was serious. To begin with, she thought I was bluffing. Then I looked at her and said, "Stop. We both know I can't handle my temper, especially when I get frustrated, so just leave." Then she knew I was serious. We had been friends for about seven years, so we could read each other.

But Jane kept giving me a hard time. I kind of got back in with that group at school, started hanging out with more people, not doing their stuff necessarily, but hanging out with them. I still had all my other friends, still hung out with them too, and all of a sudden she left me alone. I just thought it was kind of funny. If you're in a position where you know you have a lot of friends who will back you up, nobody bugs you. It's kind of like being famous. If you're famous, you can weasel your way through the courts, but if you're not, then you're toast.

The kids who don't have a lot of friends, they're the ones who usually get picked on, kids who look different. There was a Pakistani guy who got picked on. Then he got in with the right group and everybody wanted to be his friend. It's the same thing that happened with me. When people realized I was serious, they left me alone. As soon as they realized I could defend myself, they left me alone.

There was one incident which made a big difference. One day I was having a really hard time—family wasn't going well, friends weren't going well, and school wasn't going well. I got really frustrated and I punched a wall at school. I know it was a stupid thing to do because I think I cracked one of my knuckles, but I didn't cry or anything. People were like, "Whoa!" because it was loud. You could hear it at the end of the hall. People kind of looked at me afterwards like I was special. I wanted some ice to put on it because it hurt so bad. But I didn't cry. I went to class and everybody was talking about it. I still wrote with that hand afterwards.

So, a stupid thing I did out of frustration turned into people thinking I was cool. I didn't do it to show them I was tough, but still, nobody wanted to pick on me after that. And that's the way it is: you get into high school, you try to find your way into the group, and you then have to prove you're cool.

I got into home-schooling because I started skipping school in Grade 10. I can admit now that I screwed up a lot of things within a matter of one week, but at the time I couldn't admit it. One day my parents ended up actually pulling me out of school so that I wasn't around the bad influences. That way I didn't have opportunities to do what I wanted and I didn't have all the drugs and stuff at my fingertips. So they pulled me out of school and said I was going to do home-schooling. My mom tried to spend as much time with me as she could without wanting to kill me because I was a little brat.

The way I treated my mother and the way I treated my family was terrible. I apologize every day now. I can understand if they still don't forgive me just because I wasn't me. With my mom, there was a point where she didn't even know who I was. I called her nasty things, locked her out of my room, and left the house whenever I wanted to.

Oh, I had my freedom. I was the big shit. Nobody was messing with me no more. In a way, I realized from that point of view how people felt when they thought they were bigger than me and tried to pick on me. I haven't picked on anybody, but I knew I was there and I knew there was no one left to mess with me any more, so I walked around with my head held high and did whatever the hell I wanted.

It took a long time for me to realize I didn't like what was happening to me. It took several months this past year to realize that I'm not superwoman, I'm not invincible, and I've got a lot to learn. My family will tell me, sure, I've matured, but I've still got a lot to learn.

I really didn't have a life. I wasn't allowed to go anywhere, wasn't allowed to be with anyone, which was probably a good thing because I would have gotten into even more trouble. My mom gave me a journal to write in. That's probably when I started to realize that all the notes I was jotting down were just totally out there and that this wasn't me. Gradually I could see that this wasn't where I wanted to be because there was no future in it.

There are times when I'm faced with the same situation where I feel threatened and that bad attitude comes back. I had to go to the hospital to get my tonsils removed. That attitude came back in the doctor's office: I'm a shit, don't bother talking to me, don't bother messing with me, I don't want to do it. It was kind of hard to get back to the old routine and remember that there are people who are in authority who actually do care for me and want me to get somewhere. I just have to swallow my pride and live with it. But I know that whenever I'm faced with a situation where I'm threatened, it still comes back.

It's the funniest thing for me to watch because I'll get to the point where I'm starting to realize what I'm doing and I'll stand there and look at myself and say, "God, what the hell am I doing?" I probably look like the stupidest person on earth. It's going to take me a while to lose that attitude.

I have to get my education and I'm going to have to learn. It's a pity that I have to learn the hard way, but lots of people do. Lots of people sit back and watch the people who are learning the hard way, laughing at us. And now I understand why: because we thought we were the cool ones, but we're just the egotistical ones.

I act all tough, but when somebody says something nasty to me, it hurts. I have this anger problem—I'll admit it. I get these compulsive urges when people say things about me that I don't like or when they barb me. I just want to knock them out.

It's insane that somebody has to do that just to get through high school. Insane. My mom tries to relate to me about this, but she can't. She never went through that. She can't imagine some-body going to school and not being able to feel safe. It's a horrible feeling to have all those people around you, all those witnesses to stop it all, and they do nothing. You feel so insecure, so beaten and helpless. It's awful and frightening and you just want to run away. So that's what I did, I ran away from it all. But I ran to the wrong place and to the wrong things.

I did a pretty good job of staying out of jail and avoiding cops, but that's only because my boyfriend at that time wasn't letting me get into that. He was addicted to Ecstasy at one time and as a result he stutters and shakes, so he wouldn't let me touch it. I had everything at my fingertips, but he had friends to watch me when he wasn't around and keep me out of trouble. Ted and my other friends are the only reason I stayed out of trouble while I was out of school.

It's taken a lot of time and patience to change on my side and my parents', because they still have to deal with it occasionally. But like my mom says, I've really matured. I help out around the house more, I don't complain as much. You don't see me sitting upstairs with a tub of chocolate ice cream any more.

It took me a long time to find answers, especially considering that I refused to talk to people. The only person I found myself comfortable talking to was one single friend, and that was it. But if you can talk, it's good. And if you can write it down and somebody can benefit from it, that's good.

It's an emotional battle even just to think about it. It's just awful, what I put everybody through, what I put myself through, my body through. I don't even know how I got so far into it all. Here I went into high school thinking nobody's gonna change me, I'm gonna be me, and then all of a sudden my life changed. It's nice to have me back now.

I've discovered that I am not a bad artist. I spend a lot of time drawing, writing poetry, and watching TV. I spend a lot of time on the Internet, keeping up with old friends, reading articles.

I'm the youngest of six, so we are a big family. Then there were all the in-laws and all the people my mom picked up and adopted along the way. I mean, she only had so much time for each of us. I'm glad that she can now take that extra time that she spent on me and spend it with somebody else.

I don't think I could have come through it without my family. Everybody contributed in different ways. Cathy and Caroline offered me a place to stay; Angela offered me a shoulder to cry on, which I did a lot. James and Judith had their own two kids; they had jobs, a new house that really needed to be worked on, their own lives, but they offered me a place to stay. It's amazing what family will do for you.

Anybody who can defend themselves in high school is god. It's so weird. That's what things have come to. There's the violence, the sex, the drugs ... it's awful! It's just gotten 10 times worse. My mom's told me stories and I go, "You were a perfect little Catholic girl compared to us." Things have gotten really bad.

I remember if there was *ever* a fight at my old school, everybody gathered to watch. I remember some guy got rushed over to emerg because he had a broken rib, his face was all split open. Somebody stomped on him with steel-toed boots, kicked him in the sides. As soon as he was down, he was done. That's the way it is.

I don't have anything to do with the fights. I don't watch them. Everybody's curious, but why encourage it? Just being there encourages it.

There's a commercial on TV that shows there's only a bully if there are people around. The guy's yelling and it's focused on him. He's yelling, "You're such a little dweeb. Give me your lunch money," etc. Then the camera pans out and there are people playing in the background. It's an amazing commercial because it actually explains that if there weren't all those people looking to feed on it, the bullying wouldn't be there.

I guess if I could go back and do it again I wouldn't do it any differently because it's made me the person I am today. Maybe when I get older and have children I'll be able to relate with them on a personal level when they go through the same things. One thing I learned was that no matter what you do, it does always affect somebody else. I never believed that before. What happened made me understand that my mom does have a reason to worry; she's not always just trying to spoil my fun. Bad things can happen.

If I were talking to a teenager who was being bullied, I'd say, "Let it go. Whatever it is, just let it go. Walk away. It's not worth getting into. You lose too many friends and you lose a lot. Maybe you'll even lose yourself."

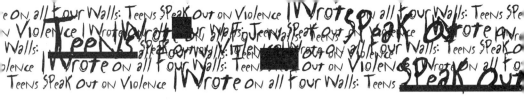

Allan

Allan, once an easy target for gay-bashers, can now define who he is, how he wants to live, and where he wants to go. He struggled with learning to accept and protect himself after a period of experimenting with drugs and heavy partying.

I came out when I was 14, just to a couple of my friends and, basically, to everyone who knew about Andrew. I came out to my mom. She was totally fine. I think she'd had some idea already. It still felt uncomfortable, though, because I was only 14 and telling my mom that I was gay. She was always OK with it. My godfather was gay, so I'd always been around gay people.

The problems started when I began high school. I went to a different school from everyone else from my elementary school. So I was the odd one out.

I got shoved into the lockers a lot by guys in the hallways. I heard people saying "Fag!" and things like that at me all the time. I remember being in gym class and getting made fun of because I wasn't as athletic as everyone and couldn't run that fast. I remember my house getting egged by people from school. That was actually what did it—when my house got egged. I just didn't go back to school after that. I didn't want to see those people, and the fact that they knew where I lived was getting to me too.

My mom and I tried talking to the principal. It was just kind of glazed over. They brought down some kid who had been telling people that I was gay. They wanted me to have a talk with him about it. I thought, Why are you doing this? Why are you parading me in front of someone who is spreading shit about me? I'd only been out for three weeks and I hadn't even told everyone in my life yet. I wasn't really prepared to "come out" to the school administration. It was just a weird situation to be in and deal with when you're 14 years old.

I was scared to go to school. I'd never experienced violence before, I'd never been in a fight. I went to an art school before. They were two completely different worlds, with completely different expectations about how you can act. So my parents and I decided I should switch schools.

It was better in the new school, but to begin with I put up walls around myself when I was there because I didn't want to get to know anyone or let anyone get to know me. I thought that what had happened at my last school would happen again, where they wouldn't want me there once they knew I was gay and they'd want me to leave. So I'd just go to school, I'd eat by myself and stay the whole lunch period in the library reading books, then I'd go to my classes, not talk to anybody, then go home at the end of the day.

Then one day towards the end of the school year I was sitting outside at lunch having a smoke and I must have looked really down on myself because this girl just came up to me and started talking to me. She was the first person who actually came up and started talking to me at school and didn't ask for a cigarette or notes for a class or anything. So I started talking to her and she invited me out to my first party. Going to that first party really opened my eyes to the fact that, even if you are the outsider, even if you are odd or different, there is still a scene, a place for you, and there are still people who are going to celebrate the fact that you are odd and different.

That's when I started partying, because I could escape from everything. It was a place where I could just be whoever I wanted to be, as gay as I wanted to be, as flaming as I wanted to be. I could wear fun fur and candy around my neck and people would say, "You look great!"

Over the summer, I switched to an alternative school because the classes were smaller and all the oddballs from the school system were there. It was more open and accepting. I didn't experience much homophobia there. I did from some people, but everyone else at the school looked down at those people. They were the ones who were ostracized for their homophobia more than I was for being gay.

The one thing about that school, though, was that I was the only out-gay person there. I'm sure there were other gays, and there were the ones who had their six-month flings being gay, but I was the only out-gay there, and I was at that school for three years. Because of that, I felt almost token-esque. Maybe people were only nice to me because I was gay. Some would ask me to go shopping with them and shit like that. It was patronizing. I don't need to be patronized.

But it was better than being ostracized. That's why I stuck it out for the time. Also, when I went there it was full of ravers. These were all people who had been in the scene for a couple of years. For me, coming into the scene was like meeting celebrities, which is kind of pretentious, but that's what raving is, pretentiousness. It's very popularity-based, just like high school, except it takes place on the dance floor.

So I started going to more parties and meeting more people, and I started doing a lot more drugs.

At that point it didn't seem to be a problem. Doing Ecstasy at that point was opening my mind to actually feeling happy and good about myself. In a way, it actually facilitated me feeling a lot more comfortable with myself. But as time went on, it did become a problem.

I was doing too much of it. I was doing a lot of different things, too. Later, it wasn't just E. I started doing crack, then I started doing crystal, then I started doing coke, and it just progressed from there. As time went on, I increased the amounts, too. I started off just doing one pill, then I was up to three pills.

There was one time, two years or so ago, when my friends and I knew we were going to be going to a lot of parties that summer, so we bought a hundred pills so we wouldn't have to keep finding more and we'd get a better deal, too. The pills were shit, though, so we had to start doing a lot of them, five or six a night. Once those pills were gone, we just kept on doing five or six pills a night of whatever pills we could get. On top of that, we'd be doing an eight-ball of K to keep us going and to keep the pills up and everything. It got out of hand.

I cleaned myself up a lot over the past summer. We stopped doing E after we got that batch of 100 pills because we could see that it was starting to get out of control. We didn't really like it any more. It didn't feel the same. We didn't get happy. A lot of the pills that were going around at that time were shit and had a lot of bad stuff in them. We replaced it with coke, though. It wasn't such a wise decision to replace something cheap with something really expensive.

I had dropped out of school by this point, so I was working full-time. I had to earn the money to feed the habit.

It wasn't like we were doing it all the time, but when we did it, we would do a lot of it. As time went on, the friends I partied with were doing it more than I was. I had started doing it before them and had introduced them to it, but later on, they were doing a ball every weekend and they just carried on. I just thought, "I can't do this any more. I can't afford to be doing this any more. I don't want to be doing this any more." I stopped hanging out with them as much. I pulled myself away from it.

I've done coke once or twice since then, but it's nowhere near the problem it used to be.

I had felt pretty safe since the gay bashing I experienced in Grade 9. Most of the time I didn't feel any aggression, but I remember two incidents at my friend Karen's birthday party.

We went to this rave. Because it was my friend's birthday and we were into the candy scene at that time, we were all really dressed up. I used to wear a lot of makeup when I went to parties like that. I was all decked out.

It was a cool party up until about two or three in the morning. I was going down to the bathroom to do some mushrooms that I'd bought from a friend. As I was eating them in the bathroom, these guys started saying all this crap to me. They were like, "Oh, you're a fag, aren't you? You really like to suck cock. Are you gay 'cause your uncle raped you? I think it's really stupid that you don't like pussy. How can you do guys? That's disgusting!" Blah, blah, blah.

The weird thing was that my friend Liam, who is also gay, was in the bathroom with me. He was a bit more butch at the party, so no one really said anything to him. He was just sitting there watching this as it was going on.

I was really high. When you're on E, things don't really matter as much, so I was just like, "Oh, whatever." I was talking back to them, kind of standing up for myself but trying to turn it into a joke because that's how I would deal with attacks like that, thinking they'd stop because it wouldn't be any more fun for them. You just have to have a winning line you can say to someone about gays, and it takes the fun out of it for them and makes them look foolish, so that's what I did. So they left the bathroom.

I went back out. I was walking to the dance floor when some guy kicked me in the back. I turned around and saw that it was this guy I knew. He was a junglist who was friends with all these hustlers and these lesbian junglists. There he was at a party kicking me in the back because I'm gay, or because I'm a candy kid, or because I'm being flamboyant or out or whatever.

I was talking to people when it happened, I didn't know what to do. I turned around and saw him laughing with all his friends. He was tweaked out on crystal, too, so I didn't want to start anything. I didn't want to go to security because I knew if I got him kicked out of the party he'd just be waiting out front after the party when there isn't security to protect me. I just ignored it for the night and did a really big bump of K. It didn't hurt that much. It was more just the shock of it actually happening. It was more of a metaphoric thing, a symbolic thing. There I was at a party that was all supposed to be about love and someone kicked me in my back. Couldn't he at least have done something to my face?

That was that. What happened that night kind of killed partying for me. I'd always thought partying was fun and safe. I'd thought the alternate world was great, where you could be whoever you were. After that, I got bitter and stopped going to most parties. If I did go, I'd only talk to my friends and I wouldn't dress up any more. I thought that if I presented myself in a different way, I wouldn't be targeted so much. It was a sad thing to have to go through because it was so much fun to dress up and do all that stuff. You can't do it, though, if it's going to make you feel unsafe.

I don't really think about bashing too much any more because I don't really present myself in the same way I used to, and the places I go, although they are straight places, wouldn't make a deal of it. I try not to think about it because if I did, it would ruin my life. If it happens and it's something little, like I'm walking down the street and someone tosses something at me, I might turn around and say, "Fuck you," but I won't dwell on it for the rest of the night.

The funny thing is that I started going to more jungle parties after that happened because I was presenting myself more as a junglist, more out. That was a funny thing, too, that it might just have all been because I was candy. Candy is thought to be really gay and I'm sure a lot of the reason junglists don't like candy kids is based on homophobia, but it's also this whole war between junglists and candy kids. I thought if I started presenting myself as a junglist—and I did like the music and everything, too—I figured if I started going to more jungle parties and hanging out with more jungle people, then they wouldn't make fun of me and I'd have all these other people behind my back who could also watch out for me. That's what happened. They did watch out for me and they did take care of me.

It's weird, because talking about all this makes me realize that I don't want to have to think about it and I don't want to live my life where you have to make these kinds of choices—but you do. I think everyone does. If I was a woman, I'm sure there are certain places in the city where I wouldn't go by myself at certain times.

These experiences open up your eyes, which makes it easier for you because you're then able to navigate better when you have a clearer idea of what's going on. You can make better decisions as to how you want to present yourself and where you want to go.

I don't really like spending too much time around my mom's house because I don't really like the area it's in and I don't feel safe there. It's kind of a weird area because there's a really old part of it that's kind of suburban, but surrounding the whole suburban area is a lot of lower-income housing, projects, stuff like that. I don't like it at three in the morning when I'm walking home. I'm always sort of shifty on the bus, concerned because you never know what could happen.

I think being out kind of helps me. When you're out, you are an easy target, but you're already saying who you are, so you won't be picked on. This friend of mine doesn't want people to know he's gay because they would put up more of a fuss and he'd get more of a reaction. I've always felt that if I am out and I say it about me before other people say it, it takes the fun away from them.

The whole gay scene is so commercial. It's so sex-based. You can't base a community on people who wear diapers and get whipped by French maids. No one else bases their community on how they like to have sex, except in the gay community. I don't think that's enough to base a community on. I've found communities outside the gay community where I feel I fit in much better.

At my work, my boss is gay and my co-worker is gay. I've worked in gay establishments with other gay guys, too. There are certain aspects I like in the gay community, but I also like to keep a lot of straight friends, mostly female, though. I like the counterbalance.

I also don't want to work out all the time. I don't want to spend all my time at the gym, picking up a guy and having sex in some bathroom. That's not really my scene.

Stuff happens and it's best just to deal with it and find out the best way to make something of your life. If I were still partying right now, who knows what I'd be putting in my nose? Who knows if I'd even have a nose left to put anything up? It's good that it got me out of that.

Partying served a purpose for me. It helped me accept myself. It helped me be comfortable being out and comfortable talking about stuff like that. Once that purpose was accomplished, it showed me that I was done with that and I was able to move on to other things.

There was a good two years where I continued to cling to it because you don't want it to die, because it was such a great thing when it first started. So I'd still go to parties and have a lousy time and bitch about the party the whole time to my friends, until I realized it was a waste of money.

Looking back now, I kind of regret leaving school because there's all this stigma about being a dropout. When I have friends that I haven't seen for a long time come up and I ask what they're doing, they might say, "Oh, I'm in college, studying psychology. What do you do?" and I say, "Oh, I work in a sex store. I do a lot of coke."

I want to go back to college because I think it gives you some credibility. It shows you can get something done, and I don't want to be stuck working at McDonald's when I'm 30. I worked at Burger King once for three months. It was really, really horrible.

I want to go to college. I don't have my high school diploma, so there's a bit of an issue, but I've been writing for two years, so hopefully I can just stick with my portfolio. I've already basically covered the first year of this class. It's like, "Please let me in. Here's a letter of recommendation from my editor ..."

Caitlin

Caitlin's early life experiences with family violence, drugs, poverty, and sexual abuse almost defeated her. But by learning who she is, Caitlin re-established an important relationship and took on a meaningful job.

My mom's family is from Italy. They moved to Red Lake and that's where my mother met my father and started dating him when she was about 19. Both her brothers had sickle-cell anemia and died. They were also heroin addicts and so was my aunt Lena. My mother got into drugs because of her brothers and sisters.

My father's father used to beat my grandmother, who was addicted to Valium. His whole family has very addictive personalities. My father was extremely abusive.

My parents moved to Toronto when my mother was probably 20-something. I was born there. They got married and it just all started.

I remember times when my dad was in construction and if he came home and there wasn't steak and potatoes on the table, it was the ultimate beating. He would drag my mom by her hair and he would hit her with pots and pans and smash beer bottles over her head.

One time they were so high they must have been hallucinating. I'm not sure what he was doing. He had a sheet on the floor and had put all the pots and pans in it and picked it up like a sack, like he was going somewhere. My mother was on the toilet. She was naked (I don't know why) and she was crying and bleeding, her face full of blood, and he's telling me to go call a cab. We didn't have a phone. I was only four or five, but I knew what he'd done was wrong.

I went downstairs to the neighbors' and knocked on the door. No one was home, so I went to the front of the house where the superintendent lived. As soon as he opened the door I said, "Call the police! Call the police! My mommy's really hurt and I need some help!" He called the cops and my dad went to jail. My mom was hospitalized and I spent the night in a foster home.

The next day, my mother came and picked me up (with my uncle) and took me to my grandmother's, where we stayed for a couple of days until my dad came back and said, "Oh, Mary. I'm so sorry! I love you," and we moved back home.

That was a regular occurrence. The beatings happened a lot. I remember the whole scene of him smashing beer bottles on her head, hitting her.

I remember one time we were in the apartment and I could hear them fighting. I was in the bedroom. I was so scared. I wasn't sure if I should pack my bags, whether we were going to Grandma's or what. I was trying to gauge the kind of fight it was, whether it was a go-to-Grandma's type or the type where we could stay home. I peeked out the door, then went out and grabbed the stereo because my dad just wouldn't stop hitting her. I pulled the stereo out and dropped it on the floor to get their attention. He took her over to the TV and took her head and smashed it into the TV. Her front teeth were dangling. Now she has false teeth because he smashed her teeth. I don't know how many times he broke her nose. She has scars all over her from him. My mom had it really bad.

I was Daddy's little girl. He never touched me. He'd always curl his tongue and put his hand up if I ever did anything he didn't like, and I'll tell you, I stopped! Whatever I was doing, I stopped because I was petrified. His hands were like weapons.

My mother decided to leave my father when I was six. That's when she met her common-law husband, Chuck, who was another abusive drug addict. They were together for 12 years. He's dead now, but I think he was a horrible person. He did nothing but bring my mother down. He would abuse her and manipulate her. She was so co-dependent she couldn't move without him. He used to yell at her "You're nothing! You're stupid!" all the time. I was always protecting my mother and he didn't like that. But something Chuck never, ever did was hit me. He wasn't sexually abusive, but he was very "touchy" for a dad. What he would do was the slapping of the ass and being very perverted with his words. You don't ask a 10-year-old what color their pubic hair is. That's disgusting. He'd even ask my friends that question, like it was any of his business. He was really disgusting and horrible.

Chuck wasn't as bad as my dad with the beatings. It wasn't as regular an occurrence. It was when they drank, which was often, but for the most part it was a little toned down. The beatings weren't as bad for my mom, but she started hitting me more. That was when the abuse really started to happen for me. Chuck would always encourage her. He'd say, "She's such a bad kid. What did you raise?"

My mom would hit me a lot. She used to grab me and pull me by my wrists. Even now, my trigger is my wrist. If anyone touches my wrist, I don't freak out, but it's very uncomfortable.

I remember one time when I asked for help with my homework. My mom said, "Well, I'm not going to do it for you." I said, "I don't want you to do it for me, I just want some help." I was stomping up the stairs. She came running up after me. I ran into my brother's room because he had a lock on his door. I tried to lock it, but I didn't manage it in time and she came after me. I was on the bed and she pulled me down onto the floor by my hair and lifted up my shirt and just gave it to me with these plastic train tracks that my brother had. I had huge welts across my back. It was really bad.

Chuck and my mom rented a house together and that's when I met Henry, the next-door neighbor. He was a friend of the family's and I thought that he could do no harm. He just seemed like a good person. He was about 47 years old.

We moved to another street, but I would still see Henry around. I was roller skating one day and I saw him and he asked me if I wanted to play Lego. I was 11. I said "Sure" when he asked me to go to his house. I went in. I had Rollerblades on, so it wasn't easy for me to get around. I went into his apartment and he locked the back door. I thought right then and there that something was wrong. I shouldn't have gone in there to begin with.

We were sitting down. I was on one chair and he was on another. He turned on a ballet movie which really, really interested me. He asked me to come over to him because he didn't have his glasses on and couldn't see to stop the movie.

I went over to him. He said, "Could you sit on my lap?" I was unsure and kind of scared, but I did. That's when he began taking advantage of me. He asked me to take my shirt off and my pants down and began to touch me. I don't know how, but I just got the courage and I ran out the door without my Rollerblades on and ran to a neighbor I had known, because we had lived on that street before, and asked her to just take me home. I was scared.

She took me to my house and I immediately told my mother everything. I said, "Something needs to be done. I'm scared. This is horrible." My mother called the police. They questioned me and took me to the hospital and Henry only actually got six months in jail for wrecking my entire life. Therefore, on good behavior, he only does three months. He did his three months and I never saw him after that. I think my stepfather had something to do with why I never saw him again.

I was having a lot of problems at school because of the abuse at home. My stepfather would beat my mother, so in turn she would take her anger out on me. It was a vicious cycle all the time, doing drugs, dealing, whatever it was. My mother was a drug addict. She was into cocaine, then heroin, then later morphine.

I went to school and they knew we were having trouble. We were really, really poor. We had absolutely no money. I used to wear bread bags in my boots because my boots would make my feet wet. We went to the food bank. When you're on welfare and your parents have a drug habit, you don't have much to live off of in the end.

There was never food in the house. We'd eat toast with butter, sprinkled with sugar sometimes. That was a treat for us. We drank powdered milk. You'd always know when my mom would say she'd been grocery shopping that day, you'd go to the fridge and there'd be nothing in it. You could always tell what she'd gotten from the Salvation Army because there would be all these plastic containers with labels on them. It was disgusting. We'd get dented cans of pumpkin pie filling.

I have a brother, John, and he's six years younger than I am and I was his mother, I raised him. I changed his diapers and made sure everything was good for him. I also took care of my mother because she'd be so high I wouldn't know what she'd do. I used to be up until three o'clock in the morning to make sure she didn't burn the apartment down. She always wanted to make these concoctions in the middle of the night. It's three o'clock in the morning and my mother's burning something on the stove and I had to make sure the stove was off and everything was cool. When she wanted to go to bed, I went to bed.

The abuse was really bad, so when I went to school I asked for help. The counselor was a male, so I refused to see him. They asked me why and I said it was because I had been abused by another man and was scared to be alone with him. They said, "There's something wrong here. How come this was never dealt with properly? Maybe we need to get Social Services involved."

That was when Social Services entered our lives. I was 11.

They didn't do much. We always made sure that when the social worker was coming over we had the house clean, food in the fridge, and we all just kept quiet, you know, everything was good at home. You don't tell anybody what's going on around here.

I stuck to that. I was really close to my mom. No matter what she did to me, she was like a god. I always loved her and wanted to take care of her and I stuck up for her.

That went on for a few years. One Christmas Eve my mom decided that she didn't want me home, so I got kicked out of the house. To this day she never told me why. I was 13 years old.

I didn't have shoes because she'd just kicked me out without my shoes on. I just stayed in the apartment building's laundry room. There were two apartment buildings across from each other. My friend lived in the next building, but she wasn't home, so I stayed in the laundry room until she came home and then I walked over with her and stayed at her place.

So it was little things like that all the time. She'd just get angry at me. I was no angel. I'd get ticked off because, if I knew she was doing something, I would confront her about it. Once I was looking for a pair of socks in my mom's drawer. I found a pack of cigarettes. I was 13 years old. I'm not going to pretend that I didn't smoke. I smoked. So I opened the pack of cigarettes and found a pack of needles and I freaked out. I asked my mom what they were and she told me that they were vitamin B pills and that they injected them into their bums. I'm not stupid. I said, "Then what's the spoon and the baking soda for in the oven?"

That wasn't the only time I found needles. I found them all around the house, a lot.

I remember a birthday party I had when I turned 12. My dad had called me. Now, throughout these years my dad was always in and out of jail. He'd go to jail for various things: break and enter, fraud, stealing cars, no license, a lot of things. So my dad called me on my twelfth birthday to wish me a happy birthday. Of course, my mom was drunk. It was an occasion to drink, right, it was my birthday. She didn't want me to talk to my dad, so I said, "OK, Mom, just let me say goodbye." She grabbed the phone out of my hand and started beating me with the phone, saying, "Hang up the phone! Hang up the phone!"

I was like, I don't understand! You have the phone in your hand. Why don't you hang it up? I don't even have the phone. How can I hang up the phone? She was so intoxicated that her mind was not there. She did this in front of all my friends.

These are examples of the kind of abuse that would go on. She broke my finger once. I was running away from her into the bathroom and I locked the bathroom door, but it didn't work, so she kicked the door in and I fell into the tub and the door came back on my finger. Of course, I didn't get it treated.

Not long after my twelfth birthday I overdosed and was taken into the hospital. I'm lucky I survived. I'm not sure what I did that night. I started out drinking vodka, straight, then I did some acid and smoked some pot. I was coming out of I don't even know where, and my friend had ditched me, and I fell down a flight of stairs, and that was when someone decided to call an ambulance, because I was lying at the bottom of the steps bleeding, choking, and puking up this black stuff—I'm not sure what it was.

I spent the night in the hospital. I try to tell people that it wasn't a suicide attempt, but if I didn't wake up I don't think it would have mattered to me. I didn't have anything. All I had was a mother that I loved so much but who didn't love me. Why she hurt me I don't know. I was the only one who listened to her, that loved her, that cared about her, that did anything for her.

I think she hurt me because she loved me. As sick as it sounds, she knew that no matter what she did to me I'd always love her, even to this day. She knew that I knew she was sick; she knew that I understood her. I don't justify it, but I understand it a little.

After the hospitalization they tried to give me counseling, but I refused. I dropped out of school for a while when I was 14. Then I decided that I needed to get my act together and that life wasn't going to be like this for me. It had to stop. So I enrolled myself back in school. School was always really important to me. No one in my family had ever graduated and I wanted to show everybody that I could do it.

I had a really strong tie with my guidance counselor and she had said to me, "Where have you been, Caitlin? What's going on?" and I told her. She said, "You know what? Maybe we need to contact Social Services and tell them. Things have to change for you. You know that it's unhealthy for you to live at home."

Then I moved into a foster home. It wasn't a physically abusive home, but there was some mental abuse in that home for sure. They'd say, "You're not going to make it. You'll never be anything." I fought it. I didn't listen to them. I just ignored them and thought, "You know what? As soon as I turn 16, I'm out of here," and that's all that I did. I got a job at the market and I'd save money and save money. Every once in a while I'd buy things for my apartment. I didn't know when I was going to have this apartment, but I knew it was going to happen.

Then, when I moved out on my own, I don't know what happened. I thought it was going to be so great. I moved into kind of a group home, semi-independent living. It was horrible, horrendous. People would be smoking pot, eating your groceries, stealing your things. It was just a big party house and that's not what I needed. I'm very much the type of person who needs structure. I need a lot of structure in my life and I need my space to do my own thing.

So I started to do drugs again. I said to myself, if I can't beat 'em, I might as well join 'em! I met my boyfriend Rusty who I'm with now. He lived in a house with three other guys who were all heavy, heavy into drugs, and that's when I started doing PCP, coke, Ecstasy. I would do three Ecstasy a night and all I could do was roll my eyes and breathe really heavily. It was so scary. I have an addictive personality just like my parents do and I couldn't stop. I would drink and I would do Ecstasy every day of the week that I could, but I could still maintain a job and go to school, so it wasn't that bad, but I sure had my fun snorting coke. But I never did poke needles. I always said to myself that I'd never, ever touch it because of my parents. They just scared me.

One day I said to Rusty, "This isn't right. This isn't who we are." I knew he was just trapped in the same thing that I was. I said, "We need to get out of here. We need to do something. We don't need to be here." So, after all the drugs and after all the "whatever else" we did together, it stopped.

A lot of this happened because I got a new social worker. He's just magnificent. He's empowering, he's beautiful. He's one of the first people to tell me that I'm wonderful, that I'm a good person, that I have it in me, and that I can succeed. That none of this other stuff is me and to stop and think about what you want. So I had a plan and I worked with him and he just listened to me, understanding me and not judging me and not wanting anything from me. That really had a lot to do with being able to change, and the fact that I wasn't happy. I didn't want to be doing drugs and having people looking at me and thinking that I was just like my mother. I didn't want to be like that.

Rusty and I got this wonderful apartment and he kept his job, worked hard, and got promoted, and I started being involved with my agency, helping other kids.

First I started chaperoning and going to conferences. I went to this one conference and met a girl who worked for Social Services and she said that even though there were a hundred kids there, I was the one who caught her eye, and that she had a perfect position for me and wanted me to work for her. I was like, oh my goodness! There were so many kids there, how did she even notice me? I've always been very active. I'm always the first one to stand up and say what I want and say what I mean and be strong about it. She really liked me and decided she wanted me to come and work for her, so I started there and it's been really life-changing. It makes me feel like I'm somebody.

My job is working for a project called the Peer Helping Project, and I'm the project leader. I travel across Ontario and I teach kids who are in care life skills. When I say life skills I mean skills that you don't learn anywhere else. I teach them what a trigger is; how to cope with a trigger; when someone's disclosing something, how to deal with it; how to be empathetic; what your listening style is and how to be a good listener, communicate, advocate for yourself; ways to help yourself with transition out of care; their rights as kids in care. That's what I do.

Foster care didn't work for me. I raised myself. I was my own mother, my own father. When they tried to put me in with rules, I couldn't deal with it. I couldn't deal with a curfew and I couldn't deal with people caring about me. I wish I could have, because I never had a chance to be a kid. I wish I could have just sat back and been a kid, but I couldn't. As soon as I got into a foster home, I had to leave. It was just too overwhelming for me.

I understand that some kids will be like that. They need to know, before they go out, what they're going out into and what it's like. I thought the grass was greener on the other side, but it certainly wasn't. There were all kinds of things, like how to pay your bills, how to be strong, how to not skip school, how to get a job—all these things. I want it to be mandatory that they take this course before teens go out to independent living. I mean, people hear about the six-ninety-six—which is what we call the independent living allowance you're entitled to once you become 16—and they think they'll get all this money and that's it. They don't realize all the boundaries that come with it.

My mom tried committing suicide in September of 2001. It was another thing that really, really changed me. I was in bed asleep and I got a phone call. It was my stepdad, drunker than you can imagine, telling me to come and say goodbye to my mom. I said, "I don't understand. What are you talking about?" He said, "Your mom's in the hospital and she's dying. You'd better come say goodbye to her."

When I walked into ICU, it felt like I'd just hit a brick wall. My mom was hooked up to every machine there is. She had a catheter, life support, and the lines ... things you see in the movies. It was like, oh my God! how did this happen? what went on? I just sat by her. She was in a coma. She had been unconscious for hours and she had aspirated, so she had puked and it had gone back into her lungs and she got pneumonia. She had overdosed on sleeping pills and methadone and another pill that I don't know the pharmaceutical name for.

The doctor said to me that he wanted me to be prepared that when my mom came out of it, she might not be the same. He said she might have brain damage due to the lack of oxygen.

She was in a coma for three days. God must have been looking over her. Those days were the hardest days of my life because I didn't know if I was even going to have a mother or whether my mother was going to be the same. It's really hard to explain the bond that my mother and I have. I have no bad feelings for her. I love her more than life itself. I would do anything for my mother. I don't know why. I think it's because it was always her and I fighting these battles.

I thought I was going to lose her. The days after she came out of the coma, she was totally wrecked. She had to be spoon-fed. She couldn't talk. It was really, really bad. If you would see her today, you'd see she made a full recovery and she's a different woman.

Chuck died a year after she came out of her coma. Ever since he died, my mother has been a wonderful person. She met another man and he's just an angel. They have a beautiful apartment together. They just renovated it all and bought new furniture. My mom's in school and drug-free.

My brother is still in foster care. He's been in foster care since I went into care, for four years. I see him. My mother actually has him for weekends. This has been a gradual thing. She used to have him for a couple of hours, then more, and now on the weekends or whenever she wants.

My brother and I have a really good relationship. I hid a lot from him. I really protected him. Nothing or no one would ever touch him. He was my baby. He didn't get the worst, but he saw me get the beatings. I tend to think that in the Italian family the boys are always favored, so he was my mom's baby and I was the black sheep. I just cleaned up after them and that was it for me.

Now that my mom is a cleaned-up woman, she is my best friend. She listens to me now. She knows what my favorite color is. She knows what things I like. She knows how I am, who I am, what I do. Before, you couldn't have asked my mom one question about me besides what my name was. She probably couldn't have even told you how old I was. Now she listens to me. We dress each other. It's like, "That looks really good" or "Chris, can I borrow that?" We have a great relationship now, but it certainly never used to be like that.

This past Mother's Day, I went into her bathroom. She has a big claw-footed tub and I drew her a bath, with bubbles, and candles everywhere. I went out and bought stuff for facials and all this spa stuff. Then I gave her a spa and a hot oil treatment for her hair. She was in the tub and I sat down and I was giving her a facial and I thought this would be a perfect opportunity to ask her why things were the way they were, so I asked her.

I said, "Mom, I don't know why and it may be hard for you to say, but why was life like this for me? Why didn't you leave? Why did you make these decisions?" The whole hospital thing was really bad, her OD'ing, and I said, first, how I'd felt about that because I never really had said before. I said, "That really hurt. That was the worst thing that ever happened to me and I want you to know how it made me feel." I expressed how much I loved her because it wasn't something we did. I told her, "I love you so much. You're so great. I know that you're a good mom and I know that you're not the person you used to be and that you want to be the person you are now and it just took you a long time."

We didn't have a long conversation. We didn't really get deep into it, but she turned around and said, "You know what?

I'm sorry. I really am sorry for everything that I did to you, and I love you." It was the first time that she'd ever, ever said sorry. It felt good. She told me she's so proud of me and where I'm going. I'm the only one in my family that has ever graduated from high school and who's going on to better things, has a good job.

I have a lot of fears now and I never really dealt with the sexual abuse from when I was 11. Even in my relationship now, it affects me. Rusty and I communicate well, but it really affects me. I'm scared and I'm hurt. I have a lot of issues now because of what happened to me when I was younger.

It's really important that if anything happens to you, get it dealt with then, because you may not realize it but when you get into a relationship where you love someone, that's when things start to come out. You feel vulnerable to the other person and you trust them and you love them and that's when all the problems start coming.

But life feels good to me. I was accepted into college, so I'm going to do a year there, then I'd like to go to the transitional year program at university. I'm going to apply for that and I have this great job with Social Services that lets me see all of Ontario. And Rusty and I love each other. That's me now. That's what I have.

Wrote On all Four Walls: Teens Speak Out on Violence Wrote on all Four Walls: Teen.
ut on Violence Wrote Out on Walls Teens Out Teens Speak Out
our Walls: Teens Speak on Wall Teen Out on all our Walls: Teens Spea
Violence Wrote on all Four Walls: Teen Out on Violence Wrote on all
alls: Teens Speak Out on Violence Wrote on all Four Walls: Teens Speak O

Kevin

Kevin's self-destructive behavior came out of the anger and frustration he felt by being singled out in school. He was humiliated and felt powerless to do anything about it.

I was born and raised in Scarborough, Ontario. It was hard growing up there because it's a very violent place. My own neighborhood was really nice, but everywhere else around there was really rough. There was a lot of gang violence and stuff like that.

I think the problems started for me when I was in Grade 5. I was always bullied because I was a small kid and they thought of me as an easy target. One day I was pulled out of my classroom by my feet and beaten by five older guys. I had never provoked these people before. They tripped me up. Then they dragged me out by my feet and started kicking me all over, in the head, in the face, in the ribs.

My teacher—he was a substitute—was at his desk, reading the newspaper, and everyone else was just kind of staring at me and laughing and stuff. I got up and started laughing with them because I didn't know what else to do. Inside I was hurting a lot because that was the first time I'd ever been through something like that.

Looking back, I'd say Grade 8 was when things got really bad. That was when I started to become very, very violent. There was a lot of bullying. They would pick on me because of my size. They'd call me names. They'd call me a loser. They rejected me. They shunned me.

From Grade 8 for four years I was severely depressed, and it all started because of this kid Colin making fun of my dad for being overweight. It was relentless, every single day, non-stop. Every single time I saw him he'd make fun of my dad. It got to the point where one day in class, he was sitting in front of me, I picked up an art stool and hit him over the head with it. I didn't really get into trouble at school because they understood what was going on. I also lied to the teachers and said he had hit me first.

A couple of weeks after, a new, really tall kid started picking on me a lot, because he saw Colin getting away with it. He came after me one day and tried pushing me down the stairs. Even then I wasn't a fighter. I was always told "Turn the other cheek" sort of thing, so I just kept walking. It was outside. I was walking with my bag and he was following me, trying to get me to fight him, calling me names and stuff like that. I broke down. I threw down my bag and I fought him. It got to the point where he kept trying to walk away because he didn't want to fight any more. I just kept hitting him and hitting him, and I was crying the entire time because I guess I was able to vent.

I went home, still in tears. I didn't tell my parents. The next day when I went to school, my teacher pulled me into the hallway and asked me what had happened. I was telling him, and I was crying even then, just telling him what had happened. I ended up getting suspended for two days because I was fighting on school property.

The anger and frustration about all the bullying was what made me cry, and the fact that I wasn't able to do anything about it. I couldn't talk to these kids. One kid actually sent a petition around the classroom. The question was, "Sign your name here if you hate Kevin." Pretty much the entire class signed it. That sort of thing chews you down so far and makes it so bad afterwards. I became very suicidal after Grade 8.

The first two years of high school were very good. I got a new set of friends who were great to me and everything was going OK. I was doing really well with my school work. Then I got in with the wrong crowd. I hung around a lot with two guys, Mike and Joe. All we would do is skip school and smoke pot. Then I decided to go homeless with some friends who had been kicked out by their parents. I went homeless with them, just for the hell of it at first. It sounded like fun.

I told my parents I wouldn't be home. I didn't tell them that I was sleeping in a stairwell. I told them I was sleeping at my buddy Bill's house. I was homeless for about two weeks. During that time there were a **lot** of fights at my school between Afghanis and white kids because the school was predominantly Afghanis (Muslims, Tamils, a lot of Hindus, stuff like that). There weren't a lot of white kids. We weren't really picked on. Just one fight broke out and then tons of fights kept going for days and days. I remember one day there were five fights in maybe half an hour, in front of the school. There were no cops. I was in every single one of them. They were like big mob fights and I was just in there, throwing punches. I liked it a lot because people gave me a lot of respect for it and I felt better about myself, I guess.

These kids that I hadn't really talked to before saw that I was a good fighter and that I was fighting with them against other people, so I was one of the crowd. I guess it's a gang mentality: you put in your work with the gang and you get respect among them.

At that time, as well, I became a skinhead for a little while. That was to fit in with the people I was hanging out with. I carried around a duffel bag with me, with a pipe, a mallet, a bat, and a knife in my pocket, a big long knife. I was getting weapons for everyone else. I would go to army surplus stores that I knew. They would give me money and I'd go buy them pepper spray and extendos and stuff like that. Even then I didn't fit in. I was just trying to find who I was, with all these different groups. In junior high I wore a bandanna in my back pocket because maybe that's who I was. But that wasn't me. I tried to be a skater. That wasn't me either. I don't know how to explain it. I guess the way you dress is who you are. That was the attitude I had because that's what I saw everywhere else.

The fights usually happened at McDonald's. There were always around 150 black guys against 150 white guys. It was really weird, all the blacks and all the whites lined up opposite each other. We'd just stand there until someone had the balls to walk up and start dissing the other people.

The last day I was homeless I brought all my weapons with me to the fight. I remember we were at McDonald's first, then the cops came. When the cops came, all the blacks started to run back to their school and we kind of chased them across the street. Tons of fights broke out.

Six of us started chasing as a group. We singled out this one guy and I was the first person to run, so I caught him. I took out my pipe and hit him in the cheekbone. I broke his cheekbone, then he put up his forearm to protect himself and I broke his forearm. He put his forearm down to hug it, then I broke his collarbone. Then I stepped back and my friends came up with their extendos, flung them out, and started beating him and beating him. I liked it. It was kind of like payback for all the bad things that had happened to me. It was bad to think that and it was a bad, bad thing to do, but at the time I didn't care. This was what I was doing and this was who I was, that's what I thought.

Then a security guard came up in a car and I guess he saw what was going on, so he yelled at the guy to get in the car, so he ran to the car and sped off. I was just standing there watching what was happening when someone came up from behind me and pushed me really hard. I fell down. I had the pipe up my sleeve so nobody else would see it. When I hit the ground, the pipe fell out. I looked behind me and it was a girl. She saw the pipe. I got up and put it back up my sleeve, then tried to walk away. She's like, "What? Are you going to hit me with that pipe? Are you going to hit me?" I said, "No. I don't hit women." I was really trying to get it through to her that I don't hit women. She kept hitting me, punching me in the face. I just put up my hands. It wasn't hurting or anything, but I still didn't want to get hit in the face. Eventually she left me alone and I had recognized an old, old friend of mine, Jamie, who was on the other side.

He's white, but he was still on their side, type of thing. He was mouthing off to one of the people on my side, who is a real big jerk. I didn't want to see Jamie get hurt or beat up because he's an old friend of mine, so I put my hand on his chest and said to him, "Jamie, it's not worth it. You don't want to start any more fights here. All your people are going away. Let's just leave it alone." I guess everyone thought that I was starting something with him, so the eight people still there just mobbed around me. Everyone was hitting me in the face. They got me down to the ground and were kicking me and hitting me.

My friends saw it while they were walking away and everyone came back and pulled me out. They had to drag me back to the school because I was so out of it from getting hit so many times. Someone found my duffel bag and brought it back to the school for me. I was the one who got messed up the most. My kneecap was smashed, I got a pipe to the back of the head and to the back. This tall guy, Ian, actually got his wrist slashed with a knife. We were all just talking to each other and I swore I was going to kill someone, I swore it. I was walking around with my knife out and I was saying to all my friends, saying, "I'm going to kill her, I'm going to kill her!" She was the reason everyone had rushed me, right?

So, after school we were all out in front of our school and the cops showed up right in front of us. We were all together in one big crowd. We all started to walk away and they said, "Where are you going?" One cop came up behind me and started feeling where I had my pipe. He said, "What's that?" and I slid it out and he said, "All right, come with me." He took me to the cruiser and asked, "Do you have any other weapons on you?" and I said, "Yeah," and lifted up my shirt, showing him the hilt of my knife. He put me up against the car and frisked me. I took out my knife for him because it was attached to my belt. He put me in handcuffs, put me in the car, took my duffel bag on his trunk, and took out the bat and mallet, and said, "Oh, man! You're the next Columbine!" We went to the station and he bragged about me to the other cops. They were all making fun of me, calling me Buffy the Brother-Slayer and The Next Columbine and stuff like that.

One of the cops came up to me and asked, "Is your dad kind of a big guy?" I said, "Yeah." He said, "Does he have a beard and used to ride Harleys?" I said yes. He said, "Do you remember me giving you rides in my cruiser when you were six years old?" I was like, oh no! He was a friend of my dad's and he's the one who arrested me.

They took me into the holding cell, then after about two hours they let me call my parents. I told them what happened. They waited for six and a half hours before the police let them pick me up.

So I was in the holding cell for six and a half hours. I couldn't sleep because everything is metal. There was a metal chair, no table. You can't sleep. All they did was give me a turkey sandwich and some milk. I don't know if you've ever tried to sit in a four-foot-by-four-foot room with nothing to do for six and a half hours? I pretty much went crazy. I was talking to myself and pacing around the room. I ripped one of the borders off the wall and cut open my finger a little bit. I wrote on the wall, "Nothing to live for, no one to die for." I don't know why they didn't see it. The writing on the wall was pretty big.

The next day, I went to the school. I wasn't allowed on the property, so I just stood on the sidewalk. The principal thought I'd come back to get revenge, but I just wanted to give Mike his wallet back. The cops came. I didn't think anything of it because I wasn't doing anything wrong. I wasn't on the property and I didn't have any weapons on me. I gave Mike his wallet. I had to start my shift at McDonald's, which was right across the street. I walked over with some of my friends.

We were sitting down, having a burger before I started work, when two cops on bikes came in and asked, "Are you Kevin Adams?" I said yes. They asked me to step outside. I was like, oh no! I walked outside and they said, "You're under arrest," and I said, "Why?" and they said, "Because you were on school property." I was trying to explain to them that I'm not a stupid kid and I wouldn't go on the property when I knew I'd get arrested for it. I said, "I don't know what you've heard, but I wasn't on the property, I only came back to give my friend's wallet back."

They wouldn't listen to me. A cruiser came to pick me up and they took me to the station again. At that point I was just kind of, "Whatever." I didn't really care. They put me in the holding cell again and left me there for nine and a half hours this time. I really snapped then. I started banging my head against the wall. I cut open my forehead with my fingernail. I just kept going like this. I wrote on all four walls, "I want to die." The writing was huge. When they came in and saw it, they took me to hospital. I stayed there for two weeks in the psych ward. Then they released me.

I was on really heavy medication that had pretty much made me a zombie, and I was taking one drug which they'd found in studies, when given to youth, produces more suicidal thoughts. That's what it was doing to me, I was becoming more and more suicidal. The combination of the two drugs was making me pretty much crazy. I was very irrational. I was very, very impulsive.

I wouldn't listen to my parents or anything. It was getting really bad for them. I was causing more and more trouble around the neighborhood. I was hanging around with the wrong people, smoking all the time, and drinking and stuff. I got to the point where I was so depressed and so suicidal that I took a knife (this is where the impulsivity comes in) and in five minutes made a plan to go to a convenience store, rob it, get the money, buy a gun, and shoot myself, because nothing else had worked. I had overdosed twice. I've tried strangling myself. I've cut my wrists so many times. I've tried drowning. I've done it all. I jumped in front of cars.

So I got a duffel bag, I got a mask, I got a helmet so they wouldn't see my hair, I got duct tape, and I got a knife. I went to the convenience store on my bike. I tried robbing them. I said, "Give me all your money." I struggled with him for a minute, then realized I could hurt him. I didn't want to hurt him. I knew the guy. He was a nice guy. So I said, "I'm really, really sorry," and I threw my knife in my bag and I ran out.

He went to the doorway and was yelling at me. There was this guy going by on a motorcycle. He stopped me and asked why the guy was yelling at me. I said, "I don't know." But he could see I had a mask on and a helmet, and a duffel bag. He grabbed me from behind and I just thought, "Whatever." I went to the ground, sat down, and waited till the cops came. I gave the cops no trouble. It was a female cop who came up to me. When I was sitting down in the car she said, "So why'd you do it?" I said, "I don't know. Just another depressed, suicidal teen."

While I was in the cruiser I started smashing my head against the window to try to break it because my hands were cuffed. I wanted to break the window so I could cut myself on the glass. The male police officer looks back at me and says, "Want a mouthful of pepper spray?" I said, "No, no, I'll stop." Then I kept doing it and I got my head through the window and they stopped the car, brushed away all the glass, then rushed me to the police station.

As soon as we pulled into the station I had managed to get my cuff off. I was trying to use the sharp part of it, as hard as I could, to pierce it through my throat, but it wasn't sharp enough, it was really dull. The female officer got out of the car to take me into the station. She saw what I was doing and she threw me out of the car, pushed me up against the car, and put on double reinforced handcuffs. They both got me by the arms and were walking me inside. I tried smashing my head off the wall. They stopped that. I was going hysterical.

They got me inside a different holding cell, one with a bed because I was supposed to stay overnight so I could be taken into court the next morning. As soon as I got into the cell and the police left, I was looking around for something to hurt myself with and kill myself with. The first thing I saw was the light fixture. It was a flat one. I got up on top of my bed and started punching it as hard as I could, but it was plastic, so it didn't break. I looked around some more and thought, "All right." I took off my sock and tried to suffocate myself with it. That didn't work either, because it was too big. So I took the roll of toilet paper and stuffed it down my throat, piece by piece.

A police officer came to check on me. It was one of the only police officers that I've ever met that actually cared. He was like, "How are you doing?" He saw my face was blue, so he rushed in, going "What the hell?" He threw me up against the wall and put a glove on because he was sticking his hand down my throat, pulling out the pieces. Five minutes later they were taking me to the hospital. I stayed there for 10 days.

After I got out of there, I was on my way to recovery. I spent six days out of the hospital, then I went to a psychiatric hospital. I was on the crisis unit for five and a half weeks. That was definitely the hardest time, the hardest point in my life that I've ever been through. One thing that happened was that I remembered being molested the year before.

I had gone to my friend Adam's place. He's 27, so he has his own apartment. I thought he was getting off work at about 7:30, so I got there about 7:15. I remember being tired so vividly. I was waiting around his apartment. His roommate was there. He seemed like a really nice guy—a forty-year-old Iranian guy. We were just talking for a little bit, and I had some grapes and stuff. He said, "So, what do you like to do for fun?" and I said, "I'm on the school wrestling team." He said, "Oh yeah? I used to wrestle," so we started wrestling in the living room.

That was going fine. He said, "Why don't we go into my room? There's more room in there." I said, "Ooo-kay." We get in his room and start wrestling again and the first thing he does is he starts to grope my testicles and my bum. I was trying so hard to keep him in a position where he couldn't reach his hand over. Even when I had this hand in a lock, he kept trying to reach this hand over. He just kept doing it.

He was a big guy. He's a construction worker. We stopped wrestling and he took off his shirt and said, "Massage me."

I said, "All right," and started to massage his arm. He said, "Take off your shirt." He started doing it to me. He wanted me to lie down on my stomach on the bed and he was massaging me some more. I was so scared. I didn't know what to do. Then he started to undo my pants. I got up and put my shirt on and I ran out the door.

I forgot about it for three days. It happened on a Thursday night. On Sunday night, around the same time that it had happened, I broke down. I started crying and crying and crying. I ran into the shower, took a shower with all my clothes on, then ran into my room. When I was in the shower I started banging my head. My mom came upstairs. She had no idea what was going on. She was getting really scared. She got my dad and my dad forced the door open. He was like, "Kevin, what's going on? Tell us." I ran into my room and crawled on top of my bed. I couldn't lie down because it had happened while I was lying down. Everything I was doing that night was just the same as what had happened three nights ago.

My parents kept trying to get me to tell them what had happened. I couldn't talk. I just kept screaming and crying. My dad kept asking me questions, like "Did you do something bad?" Finally I told him and he asked me, "Do you want me to go over there with a bat?" I said, "No, I'm not angry at him." Still I'm not angry at him, and I have no idea why.

The memory of the abuse came back to me in hospital and I was getting worse and worse. I gained about 40 pounds. They had to take me off the medication really fast because of what it was doing to me and what I was doing in my room and stuff like that. I would continuously bash my head off the walls and off the windows. I had a huge scar down my forehead for such a long time. I would sit inside the cupboard and smash my head against the wall. Once I saw the first drip of blood, I couldn't stop, I had to keep doing it. It was pretty loud, so people would rush in. There would be this huge bloodstain on the cupboard wall and I'd be bloody all over. They'd put me in restraints. Some nights I'd write on the walls, with blood and stuff, so I'd be put in restraints. I was put in restraints five times. I started to see things, hear things.

Everything started to get better after about the fourth week because of Dr. Lewis. She was a blessing. She was a psychiatrist. We talked about my violence, my impulsivity, the molestation, family issues. The only real discussion I've ever remembered is the one where she was saying goodbye to me because she was going on maternity leave. She had given me a note outlining all the things we had discussed. Not everything is black-and-white because that was one of the big things we talked about, how when something bad happens I kind of give up and just want to die because I always thought that was the easy way out. We gave each other hugs and she said goodbye and that was the last time I saw her.

When I first saw Dr. Lewis, I told her about when I over-dosed the first time. I had taken 200 Motrin painkillers and I started hallucinating. I was talking to my mom and I was yelling at her that I wanted to kill my dad. I showed her the knife I was going to use and everything. They didn't know that I had taken the pills or anything. I just went to sleep afterwards. It was in my system for four hours. I took them at eight o'clock, then went to sleep.

They woke me up to take me to the hospital for the psychiatric assessment because they were really scared. My dad was actually scared for his life! They were trying to talk to me. I was just like a zombie. I had no clue what was going on. I didn't know who I was, I didn't know who they were. I was downstairs with them. I don't remember anything that happened until they put the adrenalin into me. I was downstairs with them and they told me I had gone blind.

They got me into the car finally. They'd tried getting me dressed and stuff. I was so out of it. In the car they asked me what I was on and I wouldn't tell them. Finally I told them, but I thought I had only taken 110. I guess that's when it started to kick in and I just threw up. They got me to the hospital. They were rushing me on the gurney to the emergency room to pump my stomach.

That's when I saw the Demon. I was on the gurney and he was at my feet. My parents told me I described it to them. There was a portal behind him and he was eight feet tall, with blond hair and blue eyes. He had ridges on his forehead and pointed ears, and his name was Fack. He wanted me to come with him. I was scared. I was crying and saying sorry to everyone.

They put adrenalin in my veins and that's when I came to, pretty much. That's what I remember, them putting it into my veins. Then everything settled down a little bit. They gave me a charcoal drink and I puked that up. Because I puked up all the pills, they didn't have to pump my stomach. That was the end of that ordeal.

After the hospital, I was sent to a treatment center for youth. All the kids were a lot younger than me, like 13, 12. I had a girlfriend at the time, Samantha, and we were very, very close to each other. We liked each other a lot.

This one kid, Joey, was having a rough day and he came upstairs swearing at everyone. I was in my room with my roommate and I put my head out my door to see what was going on and he said, "Leave!" I just looked at him and closed my door. I could hear him mumbling, "Go get your girlfriend to give you head." It took me a second to realize what he had said, then I rushed out of my room in a complete rage. I walked up to him and was swearing at him. My face was beet red. I was threatening to kill him.

I was going to tear him apart, but the staff got in between us. He was scared. He was like, "He's going to kill me, he's going to kill me!" They said to me, "Is it really worth it? You're going to get charged with assault!" so I just walked back into my room and started writing poetry and I was fine with it within five minutes. That's when I knew that I was getting better. In the past, say five months previously, I would have torn him apart.

I have learned coping strategies. They are to write poetry and to work out. That's what worked for me. So whenever I was feeling really bad, I'd just ask the staff, "Can I go to the gym?" and they'd say, "Sure," so I'd go work out for an hour, come back, and I'd be fine, go for a swim or something, write some poetry. I have four or five books at home full of my poetry, and I've done a project on it at school.

I'm back in school now after missing two semesters. School's going really well for me. It's a support program for expelled students who can't get into a regular school but still want to get their credits.

I am working with a counselor on a lot of day-to-day issues, much of it to do with my anger management. She doesn't tell me what to do. She asks me what happened and I'll tell her. She'll ask me questions about it and I'll start to realize, after talking with her, what I should have done, what I could have done, what I could have thought at the time. It works with me because I know myself very, very well now.

Mary has done a lot for me, to do with court and stuff like that. I've been going to court for almost a year now. There's a court date every other week sometimes. All dealing with charges from last year. Mostly they're weapons charges from when I was homeless and getting in all those fights. Then, from the armed robbery, I have an armed robbery charge, a disguise with intent charge, and a dangerous weapons charge.

She doesn't come to court with me any more because they're all just remand dates, but she helps me before court dates because I get very anxious. My mom always comes with me. It's been hard for me lately because my lawyer doesn't even show up any more. I don't know why. He hasn't even talked to us. I have a court date coming up next week. This one's supposed to be my trial. That's why I shaved off the mohawk, because my mom kept pressuring me to. She said it would look a lot better for court.

I think recently has been the most violent period in my life. I get into fights all the time now.

My last big fight was last Saturday. I was at a place called the Brickworks. It's an abandoned factory. Me and my friends always go there to party. We make a big fire and drink and stuff. Me and my friends just scrap with each other. We don't use our fists or anything, it's just wrestling around, and I always win. That's the type of respect I have with my friends; nobody actually wants to *fight*-fight me because my name's Krazy Kevin because of all the stories.

I was really drunk. My girlfriend was with me at the time. This one kid and my girlfriend were hitting on each other and I got really mad at him. I never hit first because that way I can't get into trouble. So I was pressuring him to hit me first and he said, "Why don't you hit first?" and my friend Brian said, "Kevin never hits first. He always hits last." That pissed the guy off. I guess he wanted to prove himself to everyone, so instead of hitting me, he pushed me. He pushed me into the fire and I got second-degree burns.

I didn't know when it first happened. I'm the type of person who doesn't really feel anything when I'm drunk. So I got back up and started beating him and beating him, until I stopped. He left with his friend, Sam, and that was when the night ended. I went home with these three girls and that was it. That was the last fight I was in.

I have anger management issues. I do still fight out of anger, but it has to be a good reason. I don't walk up to anyone on the street and start a fight. I don't like to hurt people, though. That bugs me.

With girlfriends and stuff like that, I get stomped on a lot, like cheating and stuff. I've gone through so many girlfriends in the past. Since the summer I've had, I don't know, I think it's nine now. It's like a big joke with my friends now. They always say, every single time I see them, "Got a new girlfriend?" and I say, "Yeah."

I have my anger more under control now. Working out, the poetry, and knowing that if I screw up once more I'm getting sent to juvenile detention all help me. There are no holding cells, no court—I get sent straight to juvie. I can't live with that. The other guys are going to molest me there. It happens. It definitely happens. I swore to myself that if I ever get sent to juvie I'd kill myself before I got inside. I couldn't live with that. I'm not that strong a person. I know I'm not.

I hate to depend on the pills I take, but I know I have to, for now, until I can sort of do some sort of work to get through this. The impulsivity is being taken care of by the medication I'm on right now. There's a lot to deal with, but I've lived with this for so long I don't remember anything else. It's gotten so much better that, right now, it feels great for me. I've done so much work and I'm a new person now. I still get into fights and stuff, I still have my bad moments, but I'm able to get through them. I'm able to not want to die all the time. It's good. Recovery is a long, long process.

My dad may seem like a good guy, but really he's a big jerk. So's my mom. They're so much the same in that sense. They really don't care about other people. They talk trash about everyone, but the entire time they're talking trash, they're talking about everyone else talking trash. It's about how everyone else is bad. They're doing everything everyone else is doing. They're just saying they're above everyone else.

They used to be good parents when I was really young. I think things started to go downhill for us when I was about 10. My dad started to get depressed because he had been in three head-on collisions and he couldn't work any more. He gained a lot of weight, and has arthritis, and carpal tunnel, and lower back damage, so he can't work any more. So he's depressed and he's angry all the time and he takes it out on us. Not physically, but verbally, emotionally. He'll say things to us all the time. My dad talks non-stop trash to my mom and my mom talks trash to my dad.

Things are all right when I'm only there for a day, two days at the max. I've tried to go out there for an entire weekend, but it just doesn't work. I get into really big fights with my parents. And now that my dad's working again, he's always grumpy because he never sleeps. So whenever I see him, he's just a big jerk. My sisters and I can't stand having him around. He still thinks I want to kill him and that's hard for him, but that happened almost three years ago when I overdosed. I joke around about it with my mom all the time when he's not around, but it isn't a joke.

Sometimes he uses it against me, too. He'll say, if he gets into one of his hissy fits, he'll bring up things like being arrested and me wanting to kill him. Then he'll go into his self-pity stage where it's, "I know I'm just fat and stupid and worthless. You guys say that all the time about me ..." That makes me feel really bad. It's sooo uncomfortable to hear him say those types of things. He's one of the reasons, though, that I've run away in the past. Actually, he *is* the reason I've run away in the past. I used to run away all the time when I was 14 and 15, for a night, two nights, just to get away from the things he would say and the way he would treat us.

He'll talk about how I've never been a good kid, how I always wreck everything for him. One time he got me to clean the front window for him and we had a little suction-cup ornament on it to stop the birds from flying into the window. It had accidentally fallen because it had gotten wet, so it just fell off and it broke. When he saw it, he said, "You know what, Kevin? You're the reason why I want to kill myself!"

I'd like to say, "Then why don't you go ahead and do it?" but I've thought about him dying and I couldn't live with it. I realize how much I love my parents when something happens. Like my mom was in the hospital one time, she was in severe pain and she couldn't talk or she'd throw up. Nobody knew— none of the doctors or the surgeons—knew anything about what was going on. We were all very, very scared. I didn't act like it because I wanted to be the strong one in the family and help my sisters along because they were having the worst time out of everyone trying to deal with it. But I was going through just as bad a time as they were.

A couple of weeks ago I was coming home from work. There was this old guy, he was homeless, and he was pouring a whole bunch of different slushies and pops and stuff that he had found in the garbage into a big glass so he could drink it later. It depressed me so much because he looked so much like my dad. I just kept thinking about it, thinking, "What if that happened to my dad!" That scared me a lot. I realize how much I care about them when something happens.

Claire

Claire grew up in an unstable home with a paranoid schizophrenic mother. The frequent outbursts and tantrums she experienced left her feeling she had no social skills, left out in school, and unsure of herself.

My first experiences with violence started early.

I'm the baby of the family, the youngest of three. My step-sister Avril has always lived in Toronto, so I never really saw her growing up. She lived with her father. I lived with my older sister, Amy, and our parents.

Both my parents are paranoid schizophrenics. For the first four years of my life my parents were not well. They were not taking meds. They fought a lot. My dad was really abusive. He had screaming matches with my mom all the time, but then he got violent, really, really violent, physically violent, and the police were called and he was sent to jail. I was about four at that time. From there he went to the hospital. He went in and out of the hospital the whole time, back and forth, back and forth.

The violence was mostly between my parents. I was really quite protected as a kid. If there was any other screaming going on, it was at my eldest sister. I would be sent to my room, where I could hear the screaming.

I've blocked out a lot of memories. A lot of stuff has actually been told to me over the years. It got fairly traumatic at times when my mom would leave for weeks at a time and there would be no food in the house. I was only about four at the time. My sister, Amy, who is two and a half years older than me, would be trying to take care of me.

I've heard stories about when I was even a little kid—still on baby food, so I was one or two years old—and we'd be left on our own. Amy was three or four and she didn't know how to feed me, so she'd just chew up crackers and spit them into my mouth because I didn't have any teeth.

It's not so much that we were getting beaten, it was just a violent household. My parents were crazy. They didn't keep very good company. The friends who came over would also be screaming and yelling, and talking about things like smack or something. It was *that* kind of environment.

I was also very sick. I spent a lot of birthdays and a lot of Christmases in the hospital with asthma. It was a reaction to what was happening, for sure. I would like it when I was asthmatic. It was safer because my parents were nice to me then. I got ice cream and stuff. And they didn't yell at me.

Social Services was involved right from the get-go. I think I was two months old when I went into care for the first time, for a couple of months. Then I went in for another three-year stint at age five. So I did three years with a foster family, and that was an asset. My dad was in jail, I think. I don't really know where he was, but he was just not around. My mom went into a mental health facility for three years. I saw her once in the three years.

When she got out, she wanted us back and she got us back. I was 8 and Amy was 11.

I wanted to go back to my mom. I missed her. I didn't really understand what was going on. I was young and I was also really protected. I wasn't nearly as angry as my sister. Amy wanted no part of it. She just thought living with my mom was no good, but I loved my mom and I wanted to make it work. I do remember that it wasn't nearly as cool as living with the foster parents. At my foster parents' I had my own bed, my stuff, my food, my place … you know, we went to a trailer for vacations, we had like a whole family thing. We played baseball.

My mom lived in a basement apartment. She was on her meds, thankfully, the whole time, but she just couldn't do anything. She didn't get up, she didn't clean or do the grocery shopping, she didn't pay the bills. It just fell on our shoulders to do that. Well, mostly on Amy's shoulders because she was older.

My sister was essentially taking care of me. Not totally taking on *all* of the responsibilities of the house at first, but at 13 and 14 she was.

We got tired of my mother not going grocery shopping for things. She would come home with $30 worth of yogurt and liver. It was like, "Mom, what are you thinking?" How could she think it was at all appropriate? So my sister started doing the grocery shopping.

I felt really angry, and I was so *sick* of people telling me it wasn't my mother's fault, because if things sucked and it wasn't her fault, then I felt it was my fault and I was like, "Where do you get off telling me it's my fault. It's not, goddammit!"

For example, my mom had this shrink and every two months my mom would want us to go and meet with her shrink. We'd walk in and we'd instantly feel like we were being blamed for something. He would sit us down and say: "Your mother's very sick, you know, and she can't really do any better than she's doing, and I wish you girls would be a little bit easier on her and not make so much trouble."

Amy and I would just sit there silently, thinking, "Oh my God. Get me out of here! What is going on?" And when people would visit, like the public health nurses or someone like that, and they'd want to talk to us about things: "Well, these are the signs of schizophrenia and this is why your mother does this and that, and it's perfectly appropriate that she never goes grocery shopping or cleans herself or cleans the house. You shouldn't expect these things from her. This is a family unit and you need to gel with the family."

I just thought, "What the hell are you talking about? You're just going to leave me here, at 10 years old, to fend for myself because my mother's sick! Why is that my problem? No! She's just gotta get over it! No! She's just not trying hard enough and that's what it is. She's just giving up and she's having everyone help her give up."

Somehow everyone knew she wasn't being a parent, but it was never about taking us out of that home, it was only about trying to make it work for her, and it just didn't make any sense.

Then, the older my sister got, the more angry she got and so there was more fighting with my mom. They had screaming matches. I was walking on eggshells. You never knew when my mom was just going to set off on one of her rants and call you a bitch or a slut or something. And my sister was starting to remember a lot of things that happened to her as a kid. She was molested as a kid by friends of the family, I think. Anyhow, she couldn't talk about it. Plus she had to take care of me and my mom. She just kind of lost it. She started staying out late, partying, doing drugs. She was 14 at the time.

I was watching her do that. I was in Grade 7 and I was starting to get bullied at school. I didn't have any social skills when I was a kid because when my mother got out of mental hospital she never left the house and I always felt I had to mediate between Amy and my mom, so I was always the peacemaker. I would always stay at home and try to help my mother. I never really went out. I couldn't have friends over. If my friends came for a sleepover, my mom would sit in a chair and stare at them all night, and that's just *so* creepy as a kid. She'd just sit there with her tea. She just didn't get it. I don't know what her problem was, but she'd just stare at anyone who came in the door.

So, when Amy started getting into the party scene, I was getting bullied for being the loser with no social skills.

I had this friend Linda. She moved here from Toronto and she was really cool. She and I started to become friends, then all of a sudden she handed me this letter with a school picture of me with my face etched out and she started slammin' me, saying things like, "You bitch. I don't want to be your friend. You're so needy, and you flip guilt trips on me," and blah, blah, blah. She went off on me and I didn't really know how to react. I was devastated. I remember I didn't really have anywhere to go because this happened after school and I couldn't go home and be upset because I had to be really calm at home. I had to not upset my mother. It was in the winter and I ended up just sitting in the snowbank for an hour or two. I just didn't know what to do, and Amy was off partying, and I was trying to figure out how to handle it.

When Amy came home later, I asked her, "How do you make friends? How do you do that?" And she was just like, "I don't know. You just do it." So there was no one to talk to about it.

When I went back to school the next day I just tried to pretend there was nothing wrong. I just hung out with these girls who had sent me this letter, and they were totally mean to me. They said, "Claire, get lost. You're such a frigging loser. Just get away from us." I didn't know how to react. I felt defeated.

Then they started being *really* mean to me. I finally just got angry, but even though I thought I should tell them how angry I was, I couldn't. My sister was in Grade 9 and she was the coolest kid in school because she was the big partier. So I went and told Amy and Amy came and roughed them up a little bit. She didn't physically hurt them, she just bitched them out.

That was really quite powerful because she was the coolest kid in school.

I was left alone for the rest of the year and just did my own thing. Then the next year, in Grade 7, I came back with *attitude*. I was just a bitch. I was dark and I was a bitch, and then suddenly I was cool. People started wanting to hang out with me, and that was that.

At home the fighting was continuing. I was definitely in the middle. I had to take sides, so I'd side with Amy when we were together and I'd side with Mom when we were together. But I'd get angry with Amy because I couldn't understand why she was upsetting Mom.

Then one day Mom kind of lost it. Amy came home from work and she sat down with me. We were watching a basketball game on TV when all of a sudden my mom comes out of her bedroom and just started screaming at Amy about how insensitive we are and what terrible children we are and tells Amy to leave, to get out.

Amy was calm. She had a shower, packed her bags, and that was the end of her. She just walked out. She never came home.

Once Amy was gone, it sort of fell on my shoulders to deal with Mom and her outbursts and her tantrums and that whole thing. She kicked me out about six months after she had kicked Amy out. I was 15. She just said to me right out that she didn't want to be a mom any more. She said, "I don't want to be a mom. I quit!" That was it. I don't think she realized how serious this was.

I marched into the social worker at school and told her everything and said she just had to find someplace for me.

I remember going home for the first time after she had kicked me out and she was just really *numb*. After all of that fighting she was really happy to have me leave, and I just broke into tears and said, "Mom, I don't want to lose you as my mother," and she just casually said, "Well, you know, you won't. It'll be good for you to go into foster care. They have more money than I do."

I went and packed my bags and that was the end of that.

I went into foster care. I ended up moving in with that girl, Lisa, who had bullied me in Grade 6. I lived with her while Social Services was trying to find me a foster home. They couldn't find a foster home that I could gel with, so her parents ended up becoming my official foster parents and I stayed with them for about two years. I moved out when I was 17 and got my own place.

My foster home was really, really good. But Lisa was very competitive with me. She didn't really like sharing her family. She thought I should be indebted to her because she had given me this gift, sharing her family with me. Her parents treated me *really* well. They totally accepted me.

But I was very angry. I was really in a dark place. I had a lot of stuff to get over because when I lived with my mom I couldn't deal with it. It was just constantly having to be *up*, you know? I couldn't let my guard down. I couldn't have time to be angry. So when I moved in with Lisa, I took that time, and I was angry, and I was by myself a lot, and I would have hysterical fits for no reason. I felt hard done by, and cheated. That's sort of how it was.

At 17 I moved in with a roommate who was in college. I was still in high school. The age difference kind of mattered, but it wasn't a big deal. But it didn't work out and I moved out after a year.

I went to see my social worker. She was good at giving me the money but never good at giving me support. She just thought I had my shit together. So I said "I'm moving out" when I was 17 and she just said, "OK, I'll write you a check," and that was sort of our relationship. She just gave me money every month and I was going to figure out my shit on my own.

Then, at 18, in my senior year of high school, I moved to Toronto, because when I had moved out on my own at 17 I was really angry and I started using drugs, hard-core drugs. People probably would have called me an addict. I was partying, using Ecstasy, and heroin cut with Ecstasy, and crack cut with Ecstasy, that sort of thing. It made me feel I could be social. Underlying all of this was the same sort of thing I'd dealt with as a kid: I didn't feel that I had any social skills. On drugs I felt I did know how to relate to people and everyone was my best friend. I really fell into that trap. Then I overdosed one night and I never went back. That sort of snapped me out of it. I quit cold turkey. I got out of that scene and moved to Toronto.

I moved in with my stepsister, Avril, who I hadn't really seen much in my childhood because she'd lived with her dad. She's eight years older than me. It was great. We sort of started just getting it together. It was a mentoring kind of thing.

When I moved to Toronto I was starting at a new high school, so Avril helped me find a school and helped me do my homework and helped me apply for college. She encouraged me to do all that kind of thing.

She was living in this absolutely gorgeous condominium on the lakeshore in Toronto and I could rent very cheaply from her. It was very nice. I went from living like poor white trash to living the high life in Toronto. It was quite incredible.

We became very good friends. She was really helpful, not only in school but also with my sexual identity. She was one of the most gay-positive people I had ever met in my whole life. She was definitely more positive than me. I was still a bit ashamed. I didn't know what was going on or why I had these feelings or… She was just so strong and so adamant that it was OK, and just said, "You just are gay and that's OK. We love you and let's move along and find you a date." So she went out and picked up chicks with me. It was fun. It was really good.

Avril isn't gay, but she actually knew I was gay before I did. When I was 15 or 16 she was having lunch with my sister, Amy. She nonchalantly asked Amy if I had a girlfriend and Amy was like, "Why would Claire have a girlfriend? Do you think Claire's gay?" Avril said, "Well, isn't she?" and Amy's like, "Well, that would make sense—she's never had a boyfriend!"

So Avril has been really good to me. She was going to college at the same time I was. She had been a working woman but decided to quit and go back, go to law school, so while she was applying for law school I was applying for first-year college. We had a lot in common that way.

Now I'm in my third year at college, I'm 21, and I would say I've got it together. And I have a pretty good relationship with my mother now. She's very supportive of me. She was not good at being a parent and I just have had to sort of forgive her for that. I'm trying. I'm not totally over it. I still kind of have my guard up. I haven't totally accepted her. She's also become very religious.

Not only am I still resentful of how she treated me as a mother, but she and I have fundamental differences. She's scripture-holy now. I'm gay, and I live in Toronto, and I'm in college, and these are all just things that she just does not *get*, so we have a good relationship, but it's sort of an arm's-length relationship.

I have a relationship with my dad, but he's still really ill and he's still in care. That's more of a parenting role on *my* part. I go to the grocery store and bring stuff over and that kind of thing. The last time I was down I went and bought him some shoes and a coat. He didn't have any shoes. I think stuff like that is good for your soul, just to be able to get over it, or at least to *try*. I know I'm hard done by. It shouldn't have been that way, but it is, so what do you do now.

You've just got to move on. I mean, I could still be angry a lot, but that's not going to get me anywhere, so I don't really think about it much. I'm pretty detached from it all, pretty unemotional. Sometimes I can get emotional, but mostly I'm pretty level-headed. I learned that at a young age.

My sister Amy had a really hard time when my mom made her move out when she was 16 and she tried to support herself. She worked the night shift and tried to stay in high school, but high school didn't really work out. She ended up graduating, not with very good grades. She had a really hard time. She moved from place to place, got pregnant, and had an abortion. Then she moved in with our grandparents. They hit her a couple of times. Life really sucked for her. She had to go to food banks, that whole scene.

But now she lives with me in Toronto and she's in university. She found a really great partner who supported her. She went to college and took some travel and tourism courses. Now I think she's trying to be a teacher. I'm not sure what she actually wants to do. She turned it around. Me too.

rote on all four walls: Teens speak out on Violence Wrote on all four Walls: Teens
t on Violence Wrote out on Walls: Teens speak out on Violence out rote a
our Walls: Teens Wrote on all. Teens Wrote on all four Walls: Teens spea
Violence Wrote on all four Walls: Teen Out on Violence Wrote on all
alls: Teens Speak Out on Violence Wrote on all four Walls: Teens Speak O

Adam

Adam used drugs to numb the pain from being both a victim and perpetrator of violence and to escape his family's rejection. Though his experiences allowed him to learn and change, he paid a heavy price.

I never met my real father; he left when I was five months old. I grew up with my mother and stepfather. My stepfather is a cop. He's a big Jamaican guy, six foot three, and he can bench-press 450 pounds. He was my mom's best friend from the time I was about three. They started dating when I was about seven or eight, and he used to take me everywhere with him. Then, when I was 12, my first brother was born, and after that everything was totally different. That's when my stepdad started spazzing out and yelling at me a lot.

I have two little stepbrothers now; they're six and seven. But after they were born I felt like it wasn't my family any more, it was theirs: two little kids and a mother and father. Once, I asked my mom about my real father and she said, "That was the biggest mistake of my life." So I guess that meant I was a mistake too. I gave something to my mom for Christmas that said *Wonderful Mother for Two Kids*—not three, because I just don't feel like part of the family.

I guess I had a better relationship with my stepfather when I was younger, but there are lots of times when I've hated him. I felt like he stole my mom from me. I guess he took care of me, but I was blind to that. He was too strict, and he used to tell me what to do—but he wasn't my father, so I felt he had no right. I didn't respect him.

One time my mom told me to walk the dog and I said no because I was late for school. My stepfather slammed me into the wall. I hated that—there was no freakin' reason for it. He said I was being lazy, not doing my chores, but it was just because I was late for first period—music —and I loved music. On the other hand, at times I thought my mom was a bitch and I'd call her that to her face—and then he'd give me a beating for it. I took a lot of beatings at home. It's where I learned how to fight.

At school, I was bullied every day from Grade 3 through Grade 8. I got smashed so badly my nose was broken. My back was beaten with hockey sticks. In the swimming pool at the rec center four kids held me underwater until I almost drowned. I was bullied for five years straight. I think it started because I was a short, fat kid and I was new to the school. I changed schools a lot, so I was often the new guy.

I finally stayed at one school, but I kept thinking we would move again, so I didn't want to make any friends. I thought, it's going to hurt even more when we leave, so there's no point in making new friends. In the end I stayed at that school until Grade 8, but everybody hated me and I still got bullied. Then, when I was in Grade 8, I made a name for myself—when I finally started fighting back.

I had gone into army cadets at 13. I guess parents think cadets straighten kids out, but it only makes them worse. You're with a bunch of guys your own age and everybody wants to fight each other all the time. Stuff always happens. After I came back from cadet camp, any time somebody messed with me I'd pick a fight with him. This one guy said I had been talking crap about him, which wasn't true. He sucker-punched me in the face in front of my house and knocked me through the window. I caught him and stabbed him three times. I think I would have killed him. After that, I no longer cared—about my life or anybody else's. I thought, if you mess with me, you deserve to die. I started hanging around with some Hell's Angels, a bunch of guys I knew that used to run with the bikers.

I've always had a crazy relationship with my parents. My life at home was more about playing video games and RPG (role-playing) games in my room. I've played, like, 20 of them, for six hours at a stretch. I'd live my life through them. I felt more comfortable talking to my dog than talking to my parents. My dog was my best friend; I told him everything. He'd sleep on my bed and he'd growl at my stepdad if he walked into my room. He was half Labrador and half pit bull, but he never bit anybody. Even so, he was pretty big, and they gave him away when my little brother was born.

I don't trust anybody, not even my own family. I've had so many people stab me in the back. I learned not to tell my mom about my problems because she always made me feel like they were my fault. If I came home and told her I had a problem with somebody, she'd say, "What did you do?" So I never talked to her about anything and she didn't know I had problems in school. I was always depressed at home. I was always in my room, always stoned, and my mom didn't know why. She thought I was a troublemaker.

I got kicked out of the house two years ago, when I was 17. I found two drunken guys kicking a dog outside a bar. I took the dog home with me and got into an argument with my mom over it. The next day my report card came and it said I had missed 30 consecutive days of school. So my parents kicked me out.

The reason I had missed school was because of an ex-girlfriend. I had dated her for six months and I got into a lot of fights at school because of her. Nobody liked her. The last four months I was with her she was sleeping with my best friend. The day I found out she was cheating on me I did a bunch of lines of coke and then I tried to hang myself, but the bar didn't support me and I fell. As I hit the floor, another friend came in and saw me with the rope around my neck. He spent a long time with me, trying to help me out.

Because my best friend had slept with my girlfriend, I smashed him and threatened to beat the crap out of him. He had me charged with two counts of assault and uttering a death threat. After that, I got caught for possession of marijuana. I failed to appear in court, so I was put in jail for a weekend.

I even came close to getting shot once. Two guys grabbed me in the park. One put handcuffs on me—not real ones, but the kind for kinky people that you can buy in the store. They put a set of those on my arms and tied me down to a bench by the lake and dunked me. One guy held a gun to my head and threatened to kill me.

I think I was always looking for an excuse to fight. So I guess there was a lot of shit going on that led to my being kicked out of the house. Maybe it was tough love. Maybe my parents kicked me out because they knew I had to learn to make it on my own.

On the streets, at first I slept under an old apartment building. I also lived in a van for a bit, slept in a park for a while. I moved around a lot. Once, just before Christmas, I got swarmed by four guys who tried to rob me. I broke one guy's nose, and slammed the other guy, and ran from the others. But the whole incident left me really scared.

I survived on the streets by robbing crackheads. To be honest, I used to sell crack. First I'd sell it to someone and then my guys would go around the corner and rob him. They'd bring it back to me and we'd split the money. We did that for a while.

The way I saw it was, if you're a crackhead, we might as well rob you because if you spend your money on crack you're just going to waste yourself.

I used to go after drunken guys too, if I caught them hitting their wives or girlfriends. I'd get them alone and beat them up and rob them. I figured they were doing something wrong so it was OK for me to kick their butt, and robbing them was getting paid for it. As well, the people on the streets were like my family and I was going to confront anyone who hurt them. There are probably a hundred girls I still look out for, who basically consider me their big brother because I respect them and look out for them. A lot of the other guys are jealous and give me a hard time about it.

Anyhow, that's how I got money to buy food and drugs. At the time, I was doing a lot of coke too. I needed something to take away the pain. All I thought about then was that I wanted to die. So I did coke. When you're on coke, all you can think about is doing more, about where your next line is coming from. It's when you're not on it that you think about all the problems in your life.

I had experience on the street from way back, too. I was actually selling weed at the age of eight. A lot of older guys in the neighborhood knew me, so if they were selling something, they'd use me to give it to the buyer and I'd make some money from it.

I also started smoking weed and drinking around then. I started coke later, at about 12. My mom's roommate's ex-boyfriend taught me everything. He taught me how to roll joints and he got me drinking whiskey. I didn't start on beer, I started right on the hard stuff. But I've stopped drinking now. I don't want to be an alcoholic like my father.

Believe it or not, it was a crackhead that I used to smoke

with who helped me get off the streets. He let me move in with him. I was against welfare, but he said, "If you're doing something with your life and you're actually working on improving yourself, then technically you're not just using the system." So I went on welfare, which meant I had to go back and finish school. I also worked sometimes, for cash, doing renovations for a real estate agent, one of my old teachers. Every time he bought a new house that had to be fixed up, he asked me to do the renovations.

When I was first kicked out of the house I used to chill at a youth services center in the neighborhood. They let me keep clothes in the closet and food in their fridge. When they opened in the morning I'd go in, grab some clothes, wash up in the bathroom, and leave. No one even knew I was homeless. I'd tell people and they'd say, "Yeah, right. You look so clean, how can you be homeless?"

Lately I've been volunteering for them, too, by speaking to other youth about my experiences. We do presentations in school auditoriums and then we split up and go to different classes and do workshops with them. I write my own rap songs about violence and life on the streets, and I perform them for the kids and then we talk. Often kids will tell me they're pissed at someone and want to fight, and I say straight out, what's the point, when someone could get hurt or lose their life? I try to use my life experience to show them that fighting is meaningless, and I think they respect that.

The person who first allowed me to open up and talk about myself was my counselor, Paul. I met him while I was rapping to a class. He said he thought my rapping was amazing. Afterward we started talking and got into a whole conversation on religion, and we had really similar beliefs. Then he told me he was a counselor and I thought, *oh, oh* ... I had hated all the counselors

I met through youth services—but Paul was different. He also happens to be gay. I'm straight, but I was living with a gay guy and everybody had started talking about me. We had a whole conversation about gays and I guess I understood some of their struggles too.

Paul's a great guy. Sometimes I don't see him for a while, but I always go back. Or he'll call me and we'll basically have a session over the phone. He cares. He's one of the people who got me onto welfare so I could get a place. He's really been a father figure to me, more a best friend than a counselor. I can tell Paul anything. And I take his advice. I figure if he's willing to spend his time on me, then the advice has got to be worthwhile. I don't second-guess him.

I'm sharing an apartment with a friend now, but I don't feel that things are much better than when I was homeless. I'm really negative. I sometimes feel very claustrophobic. I can't sleep, so I'll be out on the streets, just walking. Or my roommate will give me antidepressants so I can crash. Sometimes I just break down and cry. It's a constant cycle for me, of dread mostly. I still wake up every morning and think, what's going to happen today?

I did have a girlfriend, Mary, and I was with her for over a year. She helped me keep going and gave me a reason to live. She helped me to have a closer relationship with my mom and step-dad. It's partly because of her that I got myself a place and went back and finished school. But I screwed up and cheated on her. She forgave me, and I really want things to work out for us, I want to be good to her, but I don't know how to do that if I can't even fix my own life.

I visit my family a lot more now. Mary and I went down and babysat my brothers when my mom had stomach flu. My mom was actually bragging about it. That made me feel good.

My brothers, Sandy and Gerry, are wonderful. Sandy is

seven years old and he's got a great sense of humor. He wants to be a fireman when he grows up, and he's always into the books. If he doesn't have any homework he'll bring a library book home and ask my mom to read it to him. I love it! Gerry is six, and he looks up to Sandy. But he's very rough and he's already gotten into trouble at school. He can't settle down. He's hyperactive, a lot like me when I was little.

I tell my mom almost everything now, and she doesn't say it's all my fault. She's starting to understand more. She told me I could move back home if I got a full-time job, but I know it wouldn't work. I don't know if I can ever live at home again, but I know I have a long way to go, a lot of changes to make, before I can think about that.

Mom used to drink a lot and smoke a lot of weed, and I know she's done a lot of other drugs in her life, but she doesn't do anything now. She won't even smoke cigarettes, except now and then when she's stressed.

I started doing drugs around the time my mom stopped. I always wondered why she got mad at me for doing drugs when she used to do it herself. I guess I had to leave home to understand that if it wasn't for quitting drinking and smoking, she couldn't be the way she is now. She used to be really depressed; alcohol does that to you. Now she's very upbeat and energetic, very responsible, and she's always working. When she gets home, the first thing she does is cook for the kids. Then she may have a couple of glasses of wine and watch a movie or read a book. She loves to read.

She wasn't like that when I was young. She used to party all the time with her buddies and then come home and just crash. I remember my mom coming home and throwing up in her bed when I was about five years old. I was crying because I thought she was sick. She used to show up with a lot of guys from the neighborhood. Most of them had known her since she was in high school, and I've known them since I was born, so they're like uncles to me. But she was into heavy drugs with these guys. I see some of them now and they're still into crack and stuff. It makes me feel bad. These are guys I really used to love. I used to look up to them.

As I said, though, my mom's clean now. She takes care of her responsibilities. That makes me feel good. And I'm trying to take the same road. That's why I quit drinking and a lot of the other things. Quitting the weed is hard, because when I don't smoke I start hearing voices in my head, and it's scary. I'm worried I might do something to someone. I'm scared of myself. That's why I don't want to fight any more either—I'm scared I might kill someone.

I used to carve myself. I still have a mark on my arm where it used to say *Mistake*. I scratched it in with a match head and a needle. On the other arm I had a heart with the word *Death* inside it, and *Life is Sorrow*. When I carved myself, it was because I really wanted to kill myself. I needed some pain. Pain allows me to move away from the crap I think about. Sometimes I head-butt walls, and once I broke a door. I've punched a wall so many times that my knuckles were bleeding. I used to have big gashes across the tops of my knuckles. I have scars from punching the wall.

I had all this anger inside me. I got myself kicked out of cadets, after going for three years, because I was so pissed at everyone. I hated everybody. When the lieutenants yelled at me, I just laughed or spit in their faces. I finally snapped—I beat up on four guys who weren't doing anything to me. They were asleep, and I flipped their cots over and started jumping on them and trying to smash their faces. And then I went and chased a guy with a knife. I don't know how many people it took to hold me down that day. I'm still always afraid of what I could do to other people.

These days I try to let my anger go into my rap music. Sometimes I feel like people are coming at me, that they want to aggravate me. I need to get away from that feeling, and I'd rather hit something, like a wall, or hurt myself than hurt someone else. I really don't want to hurt other people, but I'm always afraid I'll get to that point where I'll snap. I'm really, really afraid of myself. The counseling is another way I try to release a lot of my anger. So is smoking a joint. I always said there are three things that can keep me from fighting, keep me calm: sex, drugs—or a fight. It's true. So I'll go smoke a joint or I'll talk to somebody, but sometimes I'll just start swinging at a wall. It's all about release. I used to go to a gym and play with the punching bag, until I ripped it. I love swimming too—swimming is another thing that helps.

Someday I hope to work with kids. That's my main thing now: I love kids. All the kids know my name at the school nearby. I'll walk in with lots of junk food in my pocket for them, or I'll start a soccer game or something. All the little kids love me. I try to be a positive role model for them. I'd love it if I could do that as a job—get paid to take care of kids, maybe in a rec center or something. And taking care of other people gets me away from all the drama in my own life. It gives me a good feeling about myself.

As much as I have changed, though—getting off hard drugs, trying to stay out of fights—there are still lots of moments when I hate myself. That's been with me since I was a little kid. In a way, I've walked so far, I've taken so many steps, but I always end up in the same place.

Growing up, I always felt my mom didn't want me and I always felt resentment towards her. I know she is a good mother now, but she wasn't the best mother back then. My stepfather and I still have resentment towards each other too. The beatings I had on the street were nothing compared to what I got at home. I respect that he's a good husband to my mom and a good father to my two brothers, but I know I'll never have that kind of relationship with him.

NOW WHAT?

Advice from an **Expert**

Dr. Fred Mathews
Central Toronto Youth Services

Common to all the stories in this book is the experience of violence. For some, it began at home; for others, at school or in the community. It is easy to see how problems that start at home can play out in tragic ways in other settings.

I should state right up front that aggression is common in our society. Different forms and expressions of it can be observed everywhere, every day. Many people, young and old, have been harmed by others' aggressive behavior at some point in their lives.

Being victimized can be confusing and difficult, as the stories so generously and bravely shared in this book show. Some young people who are victimized by violence let their pain, anger, or emotions overwhelm them. When this happens, they may want to lash out and hurt others. It's difficult to predict who will resort to violence. A lot has to do with the kinds of personal supports, skills, and resources people have in their lives. Young people with positive, non-violent, and supportive friends tend to avoid creating more conflict. Having a caring adult, parent, or other family member to talk to helps enormously. Knowing how to effectively deal with conflict or feelings of anger also makes a big difference, as does self-confidence and being able to put what's happening into perspective. It's also important to be very persistent when trying to find help and to avoid situations or people that make you feel vulnerable.

Being a victim of others' aggression can make a person feel alone and scared. It can make you feel like there is something wrong with you or that you are unworthy of love, respect, or even having friends. Being a victim in one area of your life can also leave you vulnerable to further victimization in others.

Being an aggressor can be scary too. Hurting innocent people doesn't solve problems; in fact, it can make them worse. Unpleasant feelings of being out of control, overwhelmed, or not being yourself often go hand in hand with being aggressive towards others. These feelings can lead to self-destructive behaviors such as alcohol and drug abuse or putting oneself in risky situations. These behaviors may offer distractions, but they leave the original situation unchanged.

Whether you are or have been a victim of violence or are worried about your own aggressive behavior, it is important for you to know that the situation *can* change. You *can* get through this and you *do not* have to deal with the situation alone. To begin, it helps to have some understanding about violence, aggression, or bullying.

WHY DO SOME PEOPLE HURT OTHERS?

People who are aggressive or violent towards others can be either male or female, of any age, and come from a variety of backgrounds. Sometimes it is our parents or other caregivers who hurt us; sometimes it is our brothers, sisters, or other relatives. Boyfriends, girlfriends, other young people at school or in the community, or strangers can also be the aggressors.

Young people who pick on others can often be experiencing family problems, mental health issues, addictions, major life stress, or emotional troubles. Some young people who hurt others appear to be popular at school though deep down inside they may feel very insecure. They pick on others so as to feel better about themselves.

Sometimes people hurt others because of peer pressure to go along with the crowd. This pressure to fit in can push young people into involvement in gangs or anti-social groups that bully or assault others. It can be hard to resist this pressure, because the group helps a person feel safe, gives "status," and offers protection. It takes a lot of courage to resist the influence of peers.

The issue is really how to stay true to yourself in the face of peer group pressure. Hanging out with a bunch of friends isn't bad in itself. In fact, it's a normal and healthy part of growing up. People of all ages like being part of a social group whose members share similar interests or activities. The concern is how to avoid or resist pressure to engage in violent activities. Refusing to participate, speaking up to discourage aggressive members, setting an example of non-violence, and encouraging others to just walk away if things get heated up are all choices you can make.

A crowd of onlookers can also have a strong influence over a person's behavior and push them into doing things they wouldn't ordinarily do. Violence can escalate if spectators are cheering on the sidelines.

Of course, none of the explanations above excuses violent or aggressive behavior, but they may help you understand some of the reasons that motivate a person to go against his or her better judgment and harm others. If you are a victim of violence for whatever reason, it is important for you to understand that you are *not* to blame for what is happening. You may be the target of someone's frustration, pain, anger, ignorance, personal problems, or insensitivity, but *they* are still responsible for their own behavior.

Aggressors usually pick on those they think they can control or won't stand up for themselves. When confronted, some try to justify their behavior by claiming they were only teasing and meant no harm. But aggression is not the same as playful or affectionate teasing. It hurts. You know the difference by how you feel about the other person's behavior towards you or others.

Some forms of interpersonal aggression do not involve hitting or other physical behavior. They can involve threats, intimidation, name-calling, spreading rumors, gossip, or encouraging others to ignore or be unfriendly towards you. Aggression can involve mean looks or stares. Aggressors can lie to get you in trouble, steal your money or articles of clothing, or damage your personal belongings. They may pick on you because they are jealous of your accomplishments at school, your artistic or academic talents, or your physical appearance. They may make offensive comments about your family, race, gender, cultural background, language, religious beliefs, or sexual orientation.

Aggressors thrive on secrets. They depend on victims to keep quiet about what is happening to them. They pick on others because they think they can get away with it. The sad thing is, if you or no one else reports them, they *do* get away with it.

If you are bullying others for any reason, it is important to stop now and let someone help you. There are people—other youth and adults—who are trained to help you deal with whatever is going on in your life. Local social service agencies can provide you with supportive counseling, anger management skills, and other types of assistance. You can easily find them in the phone book or through a school counselor. They will not judge you and they really do understand what you're going through. You are so much more than your painful feelings; it really does take a lot of energy to stay angry. Don't hesitate to seek support. It is the best choice you can make and one that will start you down the road to turning your life around for the better.

WHAT CAN YOU DO IF YOU ARE BEING PICKED ON?

There are some very practical things you can do if you are the target of someone's aggression. First, learn as much as you can about interpersonal violence or bullying. There are lots of websites with information, personal stories, and helpful suggestions from other young people who have been there. The more you understand, the more options you will have available to try.

As a start, always try to act in a confident manner, but in a way that is true to your personality. Think about your body language. Aggressors may leave you alone if you appear confident or they think you'll stand up for yourself.

Plain old common sense will help you too. As much as possible, avoid being in areas of the school or community where you are likely to be alone. If you avoid situations that pose a risk, you can reduce the opportunities others have to pick on you. Hang out in places where there are lots of other young people and adults. Sit next to the driver on a bus; change your routines so you leave home or school at different times or take different routes; don't bring precious personal possessions or anything of great sentimental value to school or out with you in the community.

It might not always be obvious to you or others that you have become a target. Aggressors can be very sneaky about what they are doing. Trust your feelings. If you think something is wrong or people's attitude towards you has suddenly changed, take it seriously. It may be nothing, but it is always a good idea to pay attention so you can do something to stop the situation from becoming worse.

In the case of intimate relationships, if your boyfriend or girlfriend starts acting possessive and jealous, tries to emotionally manipulate you, puts you or your friends down, tries to control your life, or gets physically aggressive, ask him or her to stop immediately. If the problems persist, you must explain that this behavior is completely unacceptable and not what you're looking for in a relationship. If things don't change, then it is time to move on. Love is not about manipulation and control—period!

If it becomes obvious you are being targeted by another person, start keeping a journal and write down what is happening. Be as detailed as possible about times, places, and people involved in threatening or harming you; keep a record of all harassing phone calls to your home or cellphone; and if possible, print out hard copies of any threatening e-mails or text messages you may receive.

When others make obvious provocative comments to you, there are several immediate choices you can make: be pleasant, try to ignore it, and just walk away. If they persist, and you feel safe enough, you can confront them and ask them to stop their behavior. This might work better when you and the other person are not in front of a crowd. You can also turn the comment into a joke and laugh it off as you walk away. It can be helpful to appear to be unaffected by the comment. If you just brush off the remarks, the aggressor may be less interested in continuing to bother you. If you're not sure you'll know what to say when someone starts intimidating you, practice or rehearse some responses so you won't have to think about it in the heat of the moment. When the time comes, don't get into arguments or debates. Keep your comments short and to the point, and be firm and clear about what you want to say. If the aggressor's behavior starts to get physical or more serious, then you may want to choose other options.

Consider taking a self-defense course or learning a martial art. Just keep in mind that the point of doing this is to build your self-confidence. If at all possible, resist hitting the other person or fighting back physically; that can make the situation worse. Give them any property they are asking for as it is not worth risking getting seriously hurt over material objects. You may be able to get them back later or replace them. Don't settle scores by getting your friends to go after the aggressor. That just keeps the conflict going and can make the problem a whole lot bigger.

Sometimes young people get picked on by a group of other youth. If you know any of the group members individually and feel safe and comfortable speaking to them, approach them in private and let them know how you feel about the situation. You can ask them why they are going along with the group or tell them you are surprised by their actions. When you let them know you think they are good people, you can get them to look at their behavior. Once they know how you feel, they might refuse to join the crowd in the future or discourage others from bothering you.

Try not to be intimidated by an aggressor's threats. If they say they will harm you if you report their behavior, ignore it and continue to plan your strategy. There are a number of ways to bring their behavior to the attention of authorities that don't require you to give your name.

The most important thing is to tell someone you trust what is happening to you. You may choose to tell your parents, a brother or sister, a close friend, a relative, a teacher, a social worker, your doctor, clergy, or someone else.

If you're afraid to report your situation in person, just write an anonymous note, mail or fax a letter, or send an e-mail from a cyber café to the school or a responsible adult authority in the community. Tell them the location where the incidents usually take place; provide names and details that will help them have a thorough understanding of the situation you are concerned about.

Many schools and communities have phone lines where private anonymous messages can be left. If you want, you can ask your parents or another responsible and trusted adult to send your message. If you don't observe any helpful action resulting from your efforts, keep trying, and write or phone someone else. Many places have laws requiring teachers and principals to respond to interpersonal violence and aggression to keep schools safe. Talk to a police officer or someone else who knows what is required of school officials in your area.

Resist the temptation to avoid school or social situations because you are afraid. You should not have to sacrifice any important aspect of your life because of the aggressive behaviors of others. Just be careful, assess the situation, and get supportive people around you who can help. Tell these people what you want them to do and ask them to respect your wishes about how you want things handled. Though it may not seem like it at the time, you do have some control over the situation. It can be a very difficult and trying time, but don't give up until you feel safe and the problem is resolved to your satisfaction.

Regardless of where the violence is happening—at home, at school, or out in the community—there are people out there able and ready to support you. If you're feeling down or overwhelmed by your situation, many communities have 24-hour crisis lines that can offer support; you can find the numbers in a phone book. Contact your local youth-serving agency; they have staff who can help you deal with your situation. Some services also exist on-line to help you cope while you're working out a plan.

The bottom line is, don't be afraid to ask for help; that's a sign of strength and maturity. You are not alone; lots of young people and adults have been in your shoes and understand exactly what you're going through. Let them help you. You *can* do this!

WHAT CAN YOU DO TO REDUCE OR PREVENT VIOLENCE AND AGGRESSION?

There's a lot you can do to prevent violence. Make every effort to have friends from different backgrounds or with a variety of personal interests. You'll not only learn a lot, you will not be as vulnerable.

Refuse to engage in idle gossip and tell others you think it is unfair to spread rumors, lie, or speak negatively about people who aren't there to defend themselves. When in a group, encourage others to join in the conversation, game, or activity.

Join or start a group in your school or community that promotes anti-violence, anti-racism, or anti-homophobia. Encourage your teachers to provide opportunities to promote peer-to-peer discussion about these topics; get involved in peer support and mentoring groups; learn peer mediation and conflict resolution skills; take a younger student under your wing who looks vulnerable.

If you know other young people are being picked on, tell a teacher, principal, school social worker, or other adult. If no one listens, tell your parents, a school nurse, or a police officer. It may take a few attempts to get people to respond. Some adults, regardless of their professional background or type of job, can be insensitive to young people's needs and life experiences. If you've had negative experiences with adults in positions of power or authority, you may think or feel that you'll never be believed or get help. But don't let that discourage you; keep trying until you find someone who will believe you and take action.

The most important thing is, don't stand by and let others be harmed. If it is safe for you to do so, talk to the aggressor directly. Be a friend to the victim and let him or her know you don't like what is happening. Violence is fueled by silence and stops when we all take a stand.

CHECK OUT THESE SOURCES

We hope you find the following numbers and websites helpful. However, they are not meant to replace professional advice. Their inclusion does not constitute an endorsement by the authors or the publisher. Please also keep in mind that website content, as well as addresses and phone numbers, is subject to change.

Canada

Centre for Suicide Prevention:
http://www.suicideinfo.ca/csp/go.aspx?tabid=77

Kids Help Phone:
1-800-668-6868
http://www.kidshelp.sympatico.ca/en/

U.S.

American Psychological Association:
http://helping.apa.org/warningsigns/reasons.html

Break the Cycle:
http://www.break-the-cycle.org/

National Youth Violence Prevention Resource Center:
http://www.safeyouth.org/scripts/teens.asp